Women Against Fundamentalism

Maryam Rajavi

WOMEN AGAINST FUNDAMENTALISM

Seven Locks Press
P.O. Box 25689
Santa Ana, CA 92799

Individual Sales. This book is available through most bookstores or can be ordered directly from Seven Locks Press at the address above.

Quantity Sales. Special discounts are available on quantity purchases by corporations, associations, and others. For details, contact the "Special Sales Department" at the publishers address above.

Printed in the United States of America by

DeHART's Media Services, Inc. Santa Clara, CA

Library of Congress Cataloging-in-Publication Data
is available from the publisher

ISBN: 978-1-938115-03-5

Interior Design by Fusion Creative Works

Contents

Foreword

In this book, you will find the latest political and theological reflections on fundamentalist Islam in Iran by a very remarkable woman, Maryam Rajavi, the President-Elect of the National Council of Resistance of Iran (NCRI). In the Western world, Rajavi is known as a leading figure in the resistance against the tyrannical rule of the mullahs in Iran. She has led a career of resistance spanning decades, first within the People's Mojahedin Organization of Iran (PMOI/MEK) and now in her current role as president of the coalition of Iranian opposition groups and personalities to the Tehran regime. In her position as head of the NCRI, she has led a major international campaign to inform world leaders and public opinion of the desire of the Iranian people for change through a democratic avenue that she calls the "third option." This view holds that change should neither be brought about by war nor appeasement, but democratically by the people of Iran and their organized resistance. Rajavi is also leading the campaign for gender equality and has made remarkable achievements in this regard. As a Muslim woman, her role in this pursuit represents and poses the most serious challenge to the rulers of her country and Islamic fundamentalism driven by misogyny.

The mullahs' hysterical response to Rajavi is telling, since their official position is that no female is capable of speaking to the political, social or cultural goals of Islam. They ignore her critique of the human rights abuses and denigration of Islam by the ruling dictatorship, while simultaneously maintaining that she is both extremely dangerous and too trivial to merit notice. Given their attempts to silence this courageous woman, it is clear that her words speak directly into the heart of the current political tragedy, which continues to repeat itself time and again in Iran and the countries into which Iran attempts to project its political and ideological influence. For this reason, if no other, it behooves both those in the West who are concerned about the rise of a fanatical Islam which sponsors terrorism around the world, as well as those who are concerned about human rights – especially for women, children, and minorities – to become acquainted with Rajavi's thoughts on the experience of living under extremist clerical rule.

Born in Tehran in 1953, Rajavi's story began much like that of many other girls of that period. She was educated by a family who believed in the education of girls and attended the prestigious Sharif University of Technology where she earned her degree in metallurgical engineering. Like many other university students her age, she was horrified by the abuses of everyday people that took place under the Shah's regime. She studied various political theories and joined discussion groups while at school during this period, unaware of the cruel cost for the relatively innocent act of considering how democratic change might come about for her country. Modest to a fault, Rajavi maintains that her experience is no different from that of hundreds of thousands of others in her beloved country in that her family too suffered torture and executions under the Shah. These heinous acts continued under the new dictatorship instituted by the Ayatollah Khomeini in 1979.

What is it, we may ask, about Rajavi, her leadership and the MEK that so obsesses the mullahs and inspires democratic women around the world? After the devastating loss of so many leaders of the MEK while in Iran, and later through assassinations, how did this group, which began as "nothing special," freely reinvent itself and rise from its ashes like a phoenix? The answer is simple and relates to many of the points Rajavi makes in her writings.

Under her leadership, women of the MEK rose to the challenge of freely relearning their sense of self-awareness after years of experiencing denigration by the ruling theocracy. Rajavi has written and spoken previously of the long process of recovering the knowledge of how to be a complete person after the relentless program of propaganda aimed at women with the intention of pacifying, intimidating and creating self-doubt. Though such changes were difficult to implement at first, the women of the MEK, their mothers, sisters, daughters and friends had endured so much suffering and torture that they were willing to undertake the difficult task of achieving emancipation, self-determination and the skills of leadership.

Anyone who understands the difficult path that women leaders and scholars have had to navigate in an Islam interpreted through patriarchal and tribal misogynistic attitudes can comprehend the honor and unique position that Rajavi and other women of her ilk hold for their followers. Because women have been traditionally excluded from education – especially theological education, translation and interpretation of the Quran – feminist leaders, writers and scholars like Rajavi are both scarce and beloved. They are subjected to every kind of calumny and face incredible backlash as they make their way in the modern world.

Changes in centuries-long cultural attitudes, as well as resistance to deliberate propaganda about women's inferiority in Muslim thinking, do not simply happen overnight or by waving a magic wand over the human psyche. Deliberate policies and actions must be put in place in order to achieve such goals. This is exactly what happened in Ashraf under the leadership of women in the MEK, but most especially as articulated by Rajavi. Unlike female Muslim scholars working in the West, or more moderate Islamic countries, Rajavi has formed her thinking in the crucible of daily action by shaping the work of the resistance with respect to attitudes on gender. Female scholars in Islam are often caught between two worlds, and no one can blame them if they have taken a more neutral position in order to secure their own lives, safety and academic advancement.

Rajavi has found herself in a special situation where she has held both an activist role and a theoretical one, bringing the two arenas together to create genuine social change in gender attitudes among the men and women of the Iranian resistance. Because she does not rely only on academic discourse as a source of her authority, nor skirt the practical issues of day-to-day changes in attitudes, Rajavi presents a blend of lived theology and religious discourse which is valued precisely because it bridges the gap between theory and practice.

Those who are interested in seeing a global change in the role that religion plays in supporting systematic gender discrimination and authorizing violence against women often despair in how their programs and practices have failed to bring about their goals. This is because unless one takes up the formation and structural implications of masculinity, as opposed to simply studying versions of femininity, one is doomed to fail.[1]

The astonishing reversal of attitudes shown by the men of the MEK serves as a beacon of hope for people around the world. In a single generation of concerted action, these men have been able to change their relation to centuries' old traditions which had decreed that they are master and women are slaves.

---

1. S. C. White, "Men, Masculinities, and the Politics of Development", *Gender & Development* 5:2 (1997), pp. 14-22.

Faced with a national constitution that aims for the production of full-scale gender apartheid, Rajavi has taken on the declarations of the so-called reformers of her nation, as well as the most hardened and bigoted conservatives. She notes that, in fact, the views of both camps are essentially the same if one peels away their deceptive language. Akbar Hashemi Rafsanjani, a former President of Iran who is oftentimes mistakenly portrayed as a moderate by some in the West, is only re-articulating what Ayatollah Khomeini had written into Iran's constitution when he says:

> "... Differences in height, fitness, voice, growth, structure of muscles and physical abilities between men and women indicate that men are stronger and more capable in all these regards... The man's brain is larger; men are more rational and logical while most women are emotional and sentimental... These influence the allocation of responsibilities, duties and rights." (Chapter 2, present work)

Rajavi's leadership and experience in working with the women of the MEK completely invalidates the official ideology of Islamic fundamentalists in Iran. No wonder their universe trembles at its core when they consider what the women of the resistance have done, and how their powerful example impacts the self-esteem of the women still held captive in Iran. "Do NOT believe what you hear the Mullahs say about us," opines one young Iranian woman on Facebook in reference to the continuous slanders against the MEK and the populace's supposed hatred of them. "We love the Resistance with our whole hearts! You are our hope. Do not believe their lies!"

Rajavi is fond of citing Iran's Supreme Leader when he links the Cosmos to female agency, proclaiming, "The heavens tremble when a woman decides for herself to get a divorce!" "Well, then," says Rajavi to eager audiences of both sexes, "let them tremble! They should tremble! We will make them tremble." That her remarks are made with a combination of serenity and power, femininity and strength, is all the more of a conundrum, for such personal qualities are thought to be gendered and seldom found together in the same person. But the resistance is a movement where strong women and gentle men have deliberately formed themselves as an act of witness against their enemies. No wonder some call her "Lady of the East"[2], a Rose of Persia[3], and describe her leadership as a very special gift given to Muslims and all women. Unlike the shining women heroes confined in the House of Women in the hallowed Persian epic the Shah Nameh, her glow is not hidden by a veil like a moon whose light shines from behind the clouds.

She does not dream of legislating a religious view of life for any of her people, but rather urges the separation of religion and state in a future Iran as the only way to honor the Quran, which requires that no one should be compelled by religion.

It is in her examination of Iran's current theocratic rule that her lived experience has taken her further in understanding the role of gender politics in a Muslim society ruled by fanatics. Today's version of Islam in Iran relies on the suppression of women and their talents in order to keep its stranglehold on people. For Rajavi, gender apart-heid is not just a key strategy for Khomeini–type fundamentalists; it is essential to how they view the world and lies at the heart of their heresy. It is an emblem of their pervasive bigotry: just as Woman is to be slave to Man, so those who are not members of their clerical elite are to be enslaved by the mullahs. This includes both progres-sive and secular Muslims, as well as religious minorities within Iran, Christians, Jews, socialists, tribal entities and every other type of

---

2. Najat Abu-Bakker, journalist and member of the Palestinian Legislative Council.

3. The red rose is an important symbol for martyrs of the faith in Shia Islam.

human who does not remake him or herself in the image of their ideology.

Rajavi is not a narrow feminist or political theorist who seeks to implement a program whereby women replace men as the dominant sex, hence leading to a new form of social oppression. Rather, she understands that engaging women and men in the dismantling of gender apartheid is the only way to secure human dignity for both sexes, as well as for other countries and the world at large. Her conclusions about the way forward today are twofold:

1. Women's engagement in heated political struggle aimed at removing obstacles to equality is an indispensable imperative.

2. The subject of this struggle under the present circumstances is to confront the rising tide of fundamentalism sweeping the Middle East.

Carole R. Fontaine
Taylor Professor of Biblical Theology and History,
Internationally recognized feminist scholar

Foreword
It Can and Must Be Done

I first heard Maryam Rajavi speak about the Iranian resistance movement at an International Women's Day event in Paris in 1996. She described the oppression under which the women of Iran had been living. Following the revolution of 1979, the religious dictator Ayatollah Khomeini imposed laws that violated women's basic human rights. Women had been reduced to the status of dependents that required male relatives' permission for most of their life decisions. They remained under constant surveillance by street police when they went out in public and were subjected to brutal punishments. These laws have persisted into the present.

Maryam Rajavi presented an analysis about the nature of the Iranian regime's threat to world peace. Today, the world knows those warnings were accurate. Iran's development of nuclear weapons threatens the region's security. Its export of terrorism and ideology of Islamic fundamentalism, particularly in the Middle East, are contributing to violence, destruction and war.

Rajavi went on to explain the solution to the Iranian regime's systematic campaigns of repression and terrorism. She described the Iranian women's opposition to the mullahs' regime and their transformation into leaders of the resistance movement. As she spoke about the women's journey and their accomplishments, I realized I was in the presence of profound, revolutionary thinking about the liberation of women.

As the world debates about how to respond to the Iranian threat, they need to know about the courageous Iranian women and their heroic confrontation with the most absolute form of misogyny in the world and their dedication to overthrowing the Iranian regime. Their ideas about empowerment, leadership, gender equality and democracy rose out of the hard work of building a movement and developing a strategy to undermine the mullahs' regime. The women—and men—of the resistance engaged in self-analysis of their own gender-based thinking to discover why gender inequality persists, even in people sworn to oppose it. The first simple, yet insightful, discovery was that even women who believed in equality didn't believe in themselves enough to assume leadership roles. From that early realization, they initiated a transformation of gender-based beliefs and practices that energized the entire resistance movement.

The Iranian women also analyzed the religious dictatorship's ideology and oppressive practices and concluded that the ideas and force behind the regime's power was misogyny, the hatred of women. Rajavi once told me that the root cause of the oppression of women was sexual exploitation. It was the first time I had heard an explanation of the political power of a dictatorship based on the exploitation of women. Rajavi argues that the mullahs' control over society is based on male supremacy and gender apartheid, a term she coined. This is an original and compelling analysis of political power.

Rajavi then takes the logical, but revolutionary, step of concluding that the liberation of the Iranian people from religious fascism depends on the liberation of women, who in turn must lead the movement. Today, women are at the fore of the Iranian resistance.

I've had many conversations with the women and men of the resistance about their experiences. They or their family members have been arrested, imprisoned, tortured and executed. Many women and men have paid a high price for opposing the Iranian regime. These women have learned that freedom is not free. The resistance is not only pitted against a powerful and ruthless regime, but turbulent geopolitics has conspired to undermine them at every turn. Western governments have chosen to appease the Iranian regime by repeatedly betraying the Iranian resistance, resulting in the loss of lives, property and resources.

Yet, those in the resistance have remained organized and committed to the cause even after enduring the kinds of blows that would have destroyed other organizations. I am continually impressed by the exceptionally high standard of dedication and acceptance of responsibility they have shown in fighting the murderous Iranian rulers. Rajavi is widely known to respond to new challenges by redoubling all efforts and saying, "It can and must be done."

The Iranian resistance's analysis and hope for the future has spread inside Iran, particularly to women. They are now engaged in a political struggle against misogyny and the mullahs' regime. They are resisting daily harassment in the streets, they are participating in protests and they are organizing networks. A victory promises an end to oppression and the opportunity for equality.

The women of the Iranian resistance are the mullahs' worst nightmare. According to their male supremacist ideology, these intelligent, courageous and dedicated women leaders can't exist. Furthermore, these women pose a serious threat to their misogynous political system.

The Iranian resistance's analysis and goals are revolutionary. Their merging of human rights, gender equality and a democratic Islam is a new political and social system. They aim not only to overthrow a brutal government, but also to advocate a tolerant and democratic Islam. Their goal is nothing short of a profound social, political and religious revolution that will have a global impact.

The world beyond Iran needs these ideas and practices of creating gender equality. In countries around the world, especially Western democracies, progress has been made for women's legal rights and their participation in the public sphere. Yet, as evidenced by continuing violence against women, sexual assaults, sex trafficking and degrading pornography, misogyny is still as persistent as ever.

The Iranian women are leading the way by destroying one of the most hateful and destructive ideologies to come out of the 20th century—Islamic fundamentalism.

Rajavi believes that the 21st century will be the one that sees the full emancipation of women. She is calling on women and all democratic people of the world to unite in a front against Islamic fundamentalism.

Donna M. Hughes
Professor and Eleanor M. and Oscar M. Carlson Endowed Chair
Women's Studies Program, University of Rhode Island

Foreword
French Edition

Maryam Rajavi is a female political personality, and it is in this capacity that she has written *Women against Fundamentalism*. In it, she
lays out the major principles of her political efforts. As President-elect
of the Paris-based National Council of Resistance of Iran (NCRI),
the central body of the resistance movement that has challenged the
vicious fury of Iran's ruling regime, she attacks the pillars of Islamic
fundamentalism that have kept the regime in power, while under-
scoring the compatibility between Islam and democracy. These, and
especially the latter, are topics that are today the subjects of much
controversy.

Although a political figure, Rajavi also thinks of the complexities
of contemporary history in anthropological terms while address-
ing the basic ideological issues of Islamic fundamentalism and providing the requisite answers: "Misogyny and rejection of gender
equality in the name of Islam… constitute the motivating force of
fundamentalism."

Fundamentalists took power in Iran in 1979 after the return of
Ayatollah Khomeini to a country whose population was 98% Shiite
Muslim. Since then, it has continued to represent a "current of re-
actionary thought characterized by cruel repression, monopoliza-

tion of power, religious segregation, unprecedented misogyny and a thirst for endless expansionism."

Why did such a disastrous, misogynistic oppression emerge? Rajavi answers this question primarily in a political light: in order to preserve power. Repression of women is necessary to maintain a religious dictatorship. Therefore, in Rajavi's view, the antidote to this extraordinary evil—and in light of the inaction of states and international institutions like the United Nations—finds itself in the "forgotten power" of women. In order to defeat this devastating culture, not only do women realize that they must place themselves "at the forefront of the battle," but they must also voluntarily assume leadership of it. Thus, among the most interesting chapters of this book is the one that explains how these voluntary efforts begin and how they evolve. Rajavi analyzes the challenges and obstacles of both men and women whose personal ideas cast doubts on their capacities, thus making them fearful of assuming leadership roles. As a result of these efforts, women currently outnumber men in the National Council of Resistance.

This is the key in the struggle against the fundamentalism and extremism of the rulers in Iran. It is ingrained without political dispute and in a pragmatic way at the heart of the political and militant aspects of the resistance. Still, we are left to figure out why the regime's suppression has been built upon gender inequality.

Rajavi believes that the answer lies in the perversion of the Quran by the fundamentalists. Khomeini and his followers established a system of thought according to which there are two "fundamentally different" kinds of human beings and "this would obey a nature that follows a precise objective." Their version of social order sees the body, sentiments and identity of women as belonging completely to men. Men are the masters of women. However, after an examination of the verses of the Quran that address gender relations, Rajavi concludes that this is a thoroughly erroneous interpretation of the Quran. She believes that the fundamentalist interpretation is, in this way, deeply anti-Islamic.

For the Quran, humanity's essence lies in its conscience, freedom and sense of responsibility that is shared equally between men and women. For Rajavi, the Islam of the fundamentalists clearly betrays these tenants. Exhibiting extraordinary courage and wisdom, the author reveals that the Quran, which emerged in the seventh century, triggered positive developments in the economic and social situation of women. She refers to the Hojarat verse in the Quran, which says that human beings are created equal regardless of their gender and origins. She asks in the strongest terms: How could one respect equality and emancipation while doubting the humanity of half of the human race, as the fundamentalists do? For Rajavi, this historic achievement has been put down by an erroneous subsequent interpretation of the Quranic texts. She defends the liberating accomplishments of Islam that have thus far been hampered, and sees Islam as a religion that evolves as a result of adapting to historical circumstances.

It is to this point that I shall now turn. If it is assumed to be true that the negation of gender equality under the banner of Islam is the motivating force of fundamentalism, I will add that it is the driving force of all religions to varying degrees, according to their time and place. This is what I call "the potential for gender demarcation" as a certain universal characteristic.

It generates debate among various schools of thought, with every culture offering a view on both the male and the female. These schools are affected by the hierarchy and classification of values that continues to view males as superior to females: valiant and brave versus coward and craven, authoritative versus obedient, active versus passive, dynamic and creative versus static and stagnant, exalted versus discredited, noble versus ignoble, reliable versus unreliable, protective versus vulnerable, master versus slave, audacious and daring versus shy and reserved, among others.

This characteristic appeared in the Paleolithic era to help human beings face the riddle posed to them by the triple evidence of the persistence of the gender difference seen in all animal species, reproduction of both sexes exclusively by females and the need for prior sexual act. In the age of ignorance regarding the existence of gametes and shared responsibility in procreation between egg and sperm, the "obvious" answer to this conundrum was that males put children in females and, by extension, women are available to men so they have the fruits which they cannot deliver themselves. This certainty has continued for millennia, transformed and transmitted from generation to generation, simultaneously exchanging women by men, the confiscation of the productive capacity of women, assigning women to motherhood and mundane domestic tasks, and ultimately even confinement or the inability for women to freely control their own bodies. In this context, the world's religions appeared very recently (7,000 years for the oldest), and merely rely on these archaic and purely mental beliefs that individuals endorse as a natural truth, strengthened by notions that see sexual freedom of women in terms of a stain, a shameful act, and an attack on the male or tribal honor.

Specific methods and mechanisms were designed and implemented to ensure the continuation of this cultural and social order, reinforced by perceptions, judgments, and contemptuous "stereotypes" that are absolutely necessary to establish the permanent authority of some over others based on gender differences.

Rajavi rightly underscores the power of women. But, in my view, this is not so much because of the common nature of their gender (as the essentialist view would have it) as much as it is due to the development of a transformative individual quality, which is common to all humanity. However, due to specific cultural developments, only some (the men) have the right to cultivate and to claim this quality as their privilege.

However, if in pragmatic terms we must begin the movement towards democracy and equality by initiating a proactive sharing of power between the two genders, we must be aware: that the problem goes far beyond the scope of contemporary extremist Islam that she considers perverted; it is not certain, according to the analysis I made, that the Quran, even with its evolutionary dynamism, offers a framework for total equality between the sexes in actions and thoughts; that the difficulty is that it is not enough to achieve equality in a political opposition but it should be established as a basis of thought for the general culture and the entire population; and, ultimately, for it to be completely successful, this effort must be undertaken by all other cultures and politically elaborated states that currently exist, since this is not a debate about a particular cultural setting. It is, rather, a universal blueprint.

Rajavi offers a compelling narrative of the fundamentalist ideology, where the absolute value lays in individual sexual behavior and women are regarded as the source of sin and evil. But she stresses that out of the 6,200 verses of the Quran, only 500 of them deal with laws and regulations, including 10 "cardinal sins." For fundamentalists, sexual sin provides the essential justification for all forms of repression controlled by the Vice Squad, including humiliations, executions, ill treatment, sexual apartheid, and for women in particular: travel restrictions, dress codes, disfigurement, systematic rape in prison, trafficking of girls, aggravated prostitution, stoning, polygamy, temporary marriages, deprivation of the right to divorce and child custody, deprivation of the right to choose work and education, and naturally, deprivation, on account of their "nature" of basic legal rights (inheritance, testimony), and access to positions of power in all its forms. "A woman is deprived of the right to govern on the basis of being a woman," the Judiciary Chief of the Iranian regime, mullah Mohammad Yazdi, has written. This is while the Quranic Chapters Toba, Al Ahzab, and Al-e Omran view the abilities of "faithful and virtuous" women and men to lead as completely equal. There is even a chapter, Nur, which calls a man's slander against his wife a cardinal sin. This is an example of a situation where the Quran proactively rules in favor of women. In two useful appendices, Rajavi lists misogynist laws enacted by the mullahs who state that girls are held criminally responsible after they turn eight years and nine months (14 years and 6 months for boys) and set the legal age of marriage for girls at 13 years (and may even be earlier if the girl's father wishes). These appendices also lay out a series of answers offered by the mullahs when asked whether the UN Convention against Gender Discrimination is consistent with Islamic law. They explicitly say that equality between men and women does not conform to religious precepts (the convention was rejected in 1998). One of the mullahs even added that the freedoms granted to women are the source of "a host of evils in human societies."

Comforted by the view that even if the Quran does not provide the most ideal account of gender equality, it nonetheless offers a necessary intermediate step and even a "tactic" to move from pre-Islamic times to a new world (did the Prophet have complete equality in mind but walked a fine line when it came to realizing it?), Rajavi in a key statement expresses the principles of the resistance movement's militant action which she leads: "Commitment to the genuine spirit of Islam leads us to grant women rights and freedoms in accordance with social and economic progress of our time." Without resorting to secularism, she lists in an annex an impressive series of measures that the resistance movement proposes to achieve equality while remaining committed to Islam (a point I highly doubt, as all religions of the Book do, except to consider that this is a "tactic" similar to the one the Prophet allegedly used to move things forward without totally upsetting archaic mental habits).

After four chapters explaining this thesis, Rajavi describes the condition of women in Iran going back to 1909 and the era of the struggle of women's associations before the bloody crackdowns that began in 1979 (more than 120,000 executions, including tens of thousands of women). She then analyzes the experience of the Iranian resistance abroad, which has placed women at the forefront of the struggle, in order to oppose the mullahs' power reliance on the denial of women's identity. But she agrees that the fight must occur on two fronts: against the theocratic power and against male domination (and internalization of inferiority in female psychology).

Since 1985, the resistance movement chose to take proactive action from the top, without waiting for an unlikely change of mind or a natural increase of abilities. It began by doubling the number of women in the organization's Central Committee, by including women in all areas of specialization traditionally recognized as belonging to men (military, political decision making, and management) and by granting significant powers to women in these fields. In 1993, the movement granted women exclusive responsibility to govern the Leadership Council. One can imagine the thousands of hours of meetings and efforts that it must have taken to change the psychology of men, who perhaps felt sidelined and did not readily accept female authority, not to mention the efforts with respect to women who saw themselves through the eyes of others.

It must be admitted that there is an astonishing human experience here that we can only witness, admire and support. We must even be inspired by it since the democratic and secular appearance of this has removed domination over female bodies, the overlooking of their capabilities and their elimination on the basis of the principle of competition for power.

In a slightly different vein but with an ardor of which we grasp the full meaning, Rajavi describes the situation of Iranian dissidents living in exile in the city of Ashraf in Iraq. Deals struck between the Iranian and Iraqi governments and the near abandonment of international protections have placed pressures on them that constitute torture (we can only imagine how it must feel to be surrounded by hundreds of loudspeakers that broadcast thunderous hate messages day and night). They have been forced to relocate under some of the most unfavorable conditions to the ominously named Camp Liberty in the desert, which lacks sufficient water, medical care and any other kind of protection, while we can only hear the deafening silence of the United Nations. There, too, women are the empowered wing of the struggle.

Françoise Héritier
Honorary professor to the College of France

1

Threat of Islamic Fundamentalism

THE NOTION OF ISLAMIC FUNDAMENTALISM

In the 1960s, I was influenced by Iran's socio-political environment in the country.

Facing the repression that was imposed on the country, like many others I was longing for the freedom and prosperity of the Iranian people, while at the same time being inspired and motivated by the ideal of gender equality and those heroic women who had devoted their lives to the well-being and freedom of the people. Every news report or story made me more resolute. I especially greatly admired and liked women who had been arrested or executed by the Shah's regime, the likes of Fatemeh Amini, Mehrnoush Ebrahimi, Marzieh Oskooie and Azam Rouhi Ahangaran.

I recall that when I had just enrolled at Sharif University of Technology (called Aryamehr at the time) in 1972 and 1973, I joined ten other female students to go to the University President's office to protest against the arrest of several other female students including Ashraf Rajavi who was from the People's Mojahedin Organization of Iran. She was studying physics but was several years our senior. The Shah's secret police (SAVAK) had arrested her for her political belief.

1

As we came out of the President's office I was thinking to myself that it would be impossible for the SAVAK to release female students who had been arrested because of their membership in the opposition movements which at the time were comprised of leading groups. I was correct because Ashraf was sentenced to life imprisonment. Indeed, the SAVAK did not release her; she was only freed after major uprisings in Tehran and other cities. Ashraf walked out of prison on January 20, 1979 along with the last group of political prisoners.

I saw her on the night of her freedom. A new moving and volatile era for all of us had just begun. The new dictatorship was moving to impose itself on the fate of nation. A year later she and I became candidates in the first Parliamentary elections in Iran after the fall of the Shah. Of course, Khomeini rigged the election results through widespread fraud and violent suppression of opposition candidates as he did with the future elections. Indeed, he prevented any one from the opposition to enter the Parliament.

Several years later, in 1982, Ashraf's martyrdom during a battle with the Revolutionary Guards and showing her baby on the national television over her dead body as a booty shook the entire country.

In the 1970s, a limited number of women took part in the struggle against the Shah's dictatorship because of the nature of the struggle and the limited scope of social awareness. However, women took giant strides after the fall of the Shah. Beginning in 1980, in the early months following the anti-monarchic revolution, in my capacity as one of the officials in charge of the social section of the People's Mojahedin Organization of Iran (PMOI/MEK), I had to deal with hundreds of female university and high school students on a daily basis.

2

The tremendous energy released as a result of the revolution had inspired a generation of well-informed and motivated young people to participate in shaping the future of the country. The most unique aspect of this trend, in the context of Iran's history, was the impressive presence of women among young activists and militants. In the course of my own efforts in organizing their activities and while personally witnessing their face-to-face confrontations with Khomeini's thugs in the streets as well as hearing reports of their resistance and perseverance in prisons, which were unfortunately mushrooming across Iran, I came across a new and astounding picture of Iranian women's ascension.

Less than two-and-a-half years later, the very young girls, who had been arrested because of selling the PMOI's newspaper or exposing the misdeeds of the mullahs in the streets of Tehran and elsewhere, turned into heroines due to their resistance and perseverance under inhuman forms of torture taking place in prisons.

Hearing about their perseverance in the face of barbaric torture would make my gut wrench. I still remember the innocent faces of some of them, including Homeira Eshragh, who whispered the anthem of freedom even at the last moments of their lives.

While writing this book, I thought about them on numerous occasions, not just because each of them was like a sister to me and made up a part of my emotions and existence, but because of their quest for new horizons, their firm determination and their self-sacrifice.

The experience of that struggle, its pain and suffering has offered us an unrivaled jewel, namely women's decisive role in the struggle for freedom in Iran.

This enormous treasure trove later came to my aide, when after 1985, in my capacity as the joint-leader of the PMOI, I found the opportunity to embark on organizing the women within our ranks and transforming their positions. I must admit that during these endeavors, I learned a great deal from my sisters in the ranks of the PMOI and resistance developed a deeper understanding of the capacity and capability of Iranian women in the struggle. I was witnessing my dream of having a generation of women free of restrictions imposed by the society become reality.

I was witnessing that as pioneering women, there were teeming with inspiration and potential to engage in the struggle and make all necessary sacrifices.

The present book is a reflection of the progressive views which these women have formed in the course of their struggle. For example, as leading Muslim women, they have affirmed the central tenet of this book, namely that democratic Islam – as the antithesis to Islamic fundamentalism – guarantees gender equality.

The net result of this experience, which I believe is the most important and most ecstatic experience of my life, is that I became convinced that women are the force for change in Iran.

Years later, this reality manifested itself on numerous occasions and in many settings, including Camp Ashraf, which is an exceptional case in the contemporary world. Ashraf was an exemplary city, which those in the Iranian resistance had built through their own toil, turning it into a bastion of freedom, a short distance from Iran.

After 2003, the residents of Ashraf confronted with extraordinary difficult situation and since 2009 faced with a 4-year siege, became targets of terrorist attacks and faced massacres as well as psychological torture and an assortment of restrictions and forms of harassment. Under such complex circumstances, these women led Ashraf and conquered all the organizational, political and diplomatic challenges.

Another experience in these years was to advance the struggle for defending the legitimacy of the resistance in a complex situation including the campaign to remove the PMOI from the terrorist lists in the United Kingdom, the European Union, the United States and Canada. Much has been written about the legal and political aspects of this campaign, but few if any know that the most vital role in guiding this campaign was played by women in the ranks of the resistance in the US and Europe.

During the 2009 uprisings, too, women led the way and were on the front lines, playing a key role in advancing and organizing the protests. The fact that a young girl, Neda Agha-Soltan, became the symbol of the uprising is not a mere coincidence, but bespeaks of a new social reality in Iran.

According to official government figures, women comprise more than sixty percent of university students in Iran. Based on the latest census figures published in 2012, for the first time in Iranian history the percentage of educated women is greater than that of men. Other figures, including the decline in population growth to less than 1.3 percent, the reduction in the number of members of each household to 3.6 and the rise in the age of marriage among women to 24, are indicative of Iranian women challenging the male-dominated cultural mindset.

In reality, Iranian women have openly challenged the traditional role imposed on them by the mullahs.

These changes are important because they have occurred at a time when the ruling mullahs are adamantly working to restrict women's presence in the job market and in educational establishments. A new law adopted by Parliament in February 2013 has worsened gender segregation in the private and public spheres, while further impeding women's access to universities and education.

Nevertheless, in the midst of a horrific repression, the litmus test of women's progress is the scope of their involvement in the ranks of the struggle.

Currently, 1,000 vanguard women reside in camps Ashraf and Liberty, the bastions of perseverance against religious fascism. Women comprise more than half of the membership of the National Council of Resistance of Iran (NCRI) – the Parliament-in-exile. Tens of thousands of women have been executed or tortured during the mullahs' three-decade rule.

The fact that Iranian women have attained such stature and position amid the most complex forms of social activism, which requires a great deal of sacrifice, speaks volumes to their capacity and ability to steer tomorrow's Iran toward freedom, democracy, and lasting economic and social development.

The experience of the movement regarding gender equality amounts to a rich humane treasure trove, with all the incredible ebbs and flows faced by several generations. It can act as a guiding light for equality movements across the world, especially in the Middle East and the broader Islamic World.

Anyone who understands the qualifications of Iranian women and their potential for change would grow confident that a fundamental change is on the horizon for Iran.

Khomeini's "Islamic Republic" began with the suppression of women; and it will see its demise as a result of women's leadership.

THE MOST APPROPRIATE GOAL

The equality movement managed to earn women the right to vote by the end of the 1920s. By the end of the 1960s, the movement made significant strides in attaining greater legal equality for women. The final decades of the 20th century saw the movement struggle to remove obstacles against women's liberty and equality in various other realms.

The question, however, remains: What should be the goal of the equality movement today?

Major global developments have offered both great opportunities and considerable threats to the equality movement, namely, the opportunity to play a decisive role in shaping the future of our world and the threat of relegating the movement's status to following rather than pioneering.

A fundamental question is: What position is the equality movement seeking?

In other words, are we pursuing isolated instances of power-sharing roles and are we content with the preservation of the status quo? Are we going to be content with some mere reforms when it comes to women's rights? Certainly not!

A closer examination of the present conditions suggests a different strategy: We shall abandon this outlook altogether and live up to our role in transforming the world. This strategy demands active participation in the political struggle to remove all obstacles toward women's equality and freedom. Because the only way to realize freedom is to continuously forge ahead toward new horizons, the equality movement should not confine itself to the closed circuit of its present objectives. So, although numerous achievements have been made in the shadow of women's struggle in the past century, none of them can be considered continuous. This is because no social progress—even when it is turned into law— can be seen as permanent so long as discrimination and oppression against women continue to be the dominant culture throughout the world.

7

History teaches us that sovereign rulers never willingly give up their power and privileges. Likewise, they will never respect women's genuine rights and social status out of their own will.

At the same time, however, there is a consensus that women's participation in active political struggle is inevitable. The immediate questions arising from this consensus are: What shall be the course of women's struggle in this era? Do we have to expand the domain of our present campaigns against violence, rape and trafficking of women and children? Do we have to promote the campaigns in defense of oppressed women and for women's employment and abortion rights? Or is there another conceivable and quite different objective?

All these campaigns are very valuable. They must be continued and their activists should be honored.

The truth, however, is that while a flurry of blood, explosions, terror, invasion and poverty has shattered the lives of people in the Middle East, the equality movement is called upon to undertake a pervasive and comprehensive struggle. Today, the Middle East is burning amidst the fire of fundamentalism. The perils and flames of this ominous calamity have surpassed the Middle East to the extent that citizens of Western countries also feel its destructive fire every now and then.

So horrendous is this disaster that it leaves women very little choice: either surrender and sacrifice the achievements of humankind, especially those of the movement for equality and justice, or alternatively, rise up to fight against it with all their might.

One may ask: While women's rights and freedoms are targeted by fundamentalists in countries steeped in Islamic culture, how could this affect women in other parts of the world such as Europe and the United States?

In trying to answer this question, one can underscore the unveiled menace of Iran's fundamentalist rulers who are dragging the world towards nuclear war. It would also be helpful to note the growing trend of the mullahs' terrorism not just in the Middle East but in other countries as well. In the meantime, male domination universally benefits from the destructive currents generated by fundamentalists in Islamic communities, especially those aimed against women's rights.

The prominent American feminist, Susan Brownmiller, has touched on an important fact about violence and aggression. She believe that with every act of violence or aggression perpetrated against a single woman, the hegemony of all men in society who had nothing to do with that particular act of violence would be further strengthened. At the same time, all women in society who were not the target of that particular instance of violence would also feel further terrorized and intimidated as a result of it.[1]

This is a significant principle that enables one to understand the regressive impact of fundamentalism on the women's equality movement universally. In addition, we should note the new phenomenon of fundamentalism in Muslim communities across Western countries that has, in recent years, turned into a challenge with growing dimensions.

These issues lead to two fundamental conclusions:

First, women's engagement in heated political struggle aimed at removing the obstacles to equality is an indispensable need.

Second, the theme of this current struggle is confronting the tide of fundamentalism rising throughout the Middle East.

---

1. Susan Brownmiller, Against our will: Men, women and sexual rape, (New York: Ballantine Books,1993).

Now, has the equality movement done what is necessary in the struggle against fundamentalism? Has it assumed its pioneering role?

THE IMMINENT THREAT OF IRAN'S NUCLEAR PROGRAM

The Iranian regime represents a fundamentalist state whose survival depends on warmongering and exporting terrorism. The moment this regime finds access to nuclear weaponry will mark the beginning of a war that will rage out of control.

Let us now close our eyes and imagine we are living in 1938 on the brink of the Second World War. Let us assume that we were aware of the tragic incidents that would ensue. Would we hesitate for a moment to do everything in our power to make any sacrifice and effort necessary to prevent that war? Certainly, the answer we would all give is a resounding, "No!" We would not have hesitated.

Here again, the significance of the women's movement becomes evident. Women are the main force behind peace-seeking movements. Women have the power to block the mullahs' path towards the nuclear bomb through global campaigns. Women can also demand that their respective governments refrain from siding with Iran's fundamentalist rulers.

The day the ruling mullahs in Iran, equipped with ballistic missiles and nuclear weapons, fulfill their dominance over the Middle East, the fire of this ominous calamity will engulf Europe as well.

The mullahs and their allies assert that a war is imminent unless the world placates the regime. On the other hand, the Iranian resistance has introduced the Third Option. This solution rejects both appeasement and foreign military intervention and instead advocates regime change by the Iranian people and their resistance. Because this solution is inherently compatible with the goals of the equality movement, women have a significant role to play in it.

Let us call on all movements that advocate peace and human rights, in particular the activists of the equality movement, to support this solution. Let us urge all our sisters who work around the world to spread the peace movement, to stand up and refuse the clerical regime's efforts to rob women of the achievements of their struggle in an attempt to prolong its own rule. Together, we can prevent the outbreak of an ominous war and put an end both to a bloodbath in the Middle East and to the barbaric tyranny in Iran.

THE WEST'S APPEASEMENT POLICY UNDERMINES WOMEN'S STRUGGLE

It is necessary to bring to the attention of the global equality movement a major obstacle that is preventing change in Iran: the policy of appeasement.

How does this policy obstruct the freedom movement and the women's equality movement in Iran?

- First, by participating in the suppression of the opposition and thereby preventing change in Iran;

- Second, by opening the way for the expansion of fundamentalism and terrorism;

- Third, by providing the political opportunity the ayatollahs need to become a nuclear power;

- Fourth, by violating the law and undermining democracy and justice in Western countries.

The policy of appeasement obstructs Iranian women's struggle for freedom and equality by giving effective support to religious fascism.

If, in the distant past, there were just a few pioneering women who hoisted the flag of the struggle for liberty and equality, today there are over 1,000 courageous and selfless women. These brave women are leading a progressive movement with lofty goals and demands in the heart of a heated battle with the religious tyranny in Iran.

Although these women exist, the policy of appeasement is blocking their way. Appeasement allows the mullahs' regime to harass, injure, kill and exert tremendous pressure on members of the Iranian resistance in camps Ashraf and Liberty in neighboring Iraq. Today, these women live under the threat of expulsion or of becoming bargaining chips, and are thus compelled to tolerate an array of restrictions. The residents of Camp Liberty are currently denied protection and are forced to live in horrendous living conditions that are akin to being imprisoned.

A universal movement is needed that will rise up and defend this epicenter where the struggle for freedom and equality is in full force and, as a result, make a noble contribution to the world.

We expect that as Iranian women confront religious fascism, the free women of Western countries will also rise up against the manifestations of the policy of appeasement and against the statesmen who support the mullahs' religious dictatorship. This is a humanitarian, ethical and democratic obligation, since anyone engaged in the policy of appeasement is directly involved in solidifying the pillars of religious tyranny in Iran and thereby in the spread of terrorism and fundamentalism.

For years, these governments officially stated that the blacklisting of the Iranian opposition had been intended to comply with the demands of the Iranian regime. They even defied European and British court rulings that called for the removal of this designation for three years until finally our resistance managed, through an extensive political and legal campaign, to compel these governments to delist the PMOI. Nonetheless, many key EU member states continue to espouse policies that impose various blockades against the Iranian resistance movement. In the United States, the State Department continued to keep the Iranian resistance on its blacklist, without substantive evidence or legal basis, in order to avoid upsetting its relations with Tehran's ruling mullahs. But, it, too, was compelled to delist the PMOI in September 2012 on the basis of a federal court of appeals ruling.

Activists of the equality movement worldwide must reject this violation of the fundamental values of the West by collusions that further strengthen fundamentalism. They must join hands and stand united against authoritarian governments and institutions that are working to imperil the achievements of humanity and particularly the accomplishments of women. Indeed, once Iran's dictatorship is compelled to give its place to the rule of freedom and democracy, and once Iranian women gain freedom and equality, the worldwide equality movement will take a major leap forward.

ARAB SPRING

The uprisings in the Middle East and North Africa have signaled the desire for freedom and equality for the people in those regions. These movements have grown out of a fundamental conflict.

In reality, societies in that part of the world require a set of relationships based on freedom and democracy for the sake of advancement and evolution. Yet, the stubborn dictatorships, which cannot rule without repression and terror, have blocked their path.

The leader of the Iranian resistance, Massoud Rajavi, has said: "The path to industrial growth and capitalism in these countries, without political freedoms—indispensable to the path of economic and social development—has reached a dead end. The pre-capitalist, fundamentalist regime in Iran has put up this blockade far more than others, for which reason the alarms over its overthrow have begun to sound."

I must emphasize that these movements, by their nature and in their essence, are anti-fundamentalist. Nevertheless, with the overthrow of tyrannies, they run the risk of being derailed by the fundamentalists.

To quash the Arab Spring once and for all, the mullahs have been waiting in the wings with the sinister motto of "Islamic awakening." In Iran, the mullahs have reached a roadblock, and in order to maintain power, they need to take the fate of the Arab Spring hostage.

For this reason, many warily asked: "Will these revolutions culminate in the fundamentalists ascending to power, as happened in Iran 33 years ago? And will the women who have so courageously taken part in the uprisings not become its biggest losers?"

Is the ultimate fate of our nations anything other than dictatorships or theocracies?

Have the struggles for change and the movements for freedom reached a deadlock?

No. It is never that way.

Why?

Because today we have an answer; one that offers a breakthrough for freedom and equality. It is an option that steers society toward genuine progress and development.

This answer is women's assumption of responsibility and their active participation and leadership.

Allow me to refer to the experience of the Iranian revolution. While the revolution was stolen by Khomeini, a magnificent resistance emerged to challenge it. This resistance heralds freedom and democracy for Iran's future and hinges on women's leadership roles.

Fundamentalists begin with the oppression and degradation of women in order to erect the pillars of their power. Nevertheless, the struggle and the uprising involving these very oppressed women will undoubtedly result in the defeat of fundamentalism.

This reality is the essence of what our resistance movement has gone through. This experience proves that as the struggle to attain freedom and democracy becomes more difficult, and the face-off with religious fundamentalism becomes more profound, gender equality and women's participation in the struggle, particularly their leadership roles, becomes more indispensable.

Here, I want to elaborate on what women's leadership means in practice and what its outcomes have been thus far.

Does it mean that men are marginalized and only women should carry out the resistance?

Does it mean that men have to hand over the management of the resistance movement to women?

No, not at all! This phenomenon has neither come to eliminate others, nor compete with the existing status quo. But, it is seeking to build a set of relationships based on freedom, equality and democracy.

For this reason, in the resistance movement led by women, men have not been marginalized. To the contrary, they have become more emancipated and responsible while remaining more resolved in the struggle for freedom. For women's assumption of responsibility rests on free choice and expression, as well as on their genuine participation alongside men.

Isn't the most urgent and necessary response to the problem of youths their participation in all aspects of society's economic and political undertakings?

So, an alternative approach is needed that would guarantee women's genuine participation; a set of relationships based on taking into account and hearing out the people; a set of relationships based on tolerance and lenience. Thus, women are the answer.

INTERNATIONAL SOLIDARITY

Today, a common menace threatens not only Iranian women, but also our sisters in Iraq, Lebanon, Egypt, Somalia, Afghanistan and elsewhere. Hence, a united front is indispensable against fundamentalism and the policy of appeasement. The activities of the women's movement are not meant to be merely complementary in the struggle against fundamentalism. Rather, without the pioneering role of women, overcoming this demon will be impossible.

This is one of the greatest urgencies of our time. We live in an era where the solutions and approaches that support and reinforce the male-dominated regime have reached their demise while a new solution founded on values offered by equality is needed. Women have an enormous and as yet untapped potential to affect changes in the world that herlad freedom and equality. This noble capacity will lead human society to genuine freedom.

When women rise up to partake in this battle, they tend to discover their forgotten powers. We can only realize our real powers when we engage in a serious struggle. This is the path that leads to new opportunities and rebirths. It is on this path that women overcome the destructive skepticism of their own might and find out that not only are they worthy of this struggle, but it is they who are the guides and leaders towards freedom.

Bearing this outlook, we can answer the primary question: Does the world need the equality movement to engage in the broad-based realm of the struggle against fundamentalism?

The answer is yes, because women form the primary force of struggle against fundamentalism. Without their participation, the world would not be able to overcome the danger that threatens mankind. The heart of the matter is that the defeat of fundamentalism will be realized only through women's leadership.

The equality movement forms the source of our power and unity in an active and organized struggle. This is a movement that heightens the flames of resistance and returns dignity and noble values to human life. This movement is today's force for advancement and victory and holds tomorrow's promises. So, let us rise up together for the sake of our common ideals and historic responsibilities. This is our duty; it is within our powers and it is what both present and future generations expect from us.

THE WAY TO DEFEAT FUNDAMENTALISM

How can we defeat fundamentalism and misogyny? How can we prevent the burial of democracy in countries under the influence of fundamentalism? The answer lies in women's leadership. If one seeks to eliminate the culture of male-dominance as one that is inhuman, one must destroy it in its entirety. Accordingly, the establishment of democracy is impossible without women playing an active role in political leadership. Otherwise, any hypothetical progress would be reversible.

When we envision the prospects of this cause and the struggle we are engaged in for equality, we see horizons where we can turn today's darkness into brightness while breaking the chains and attaining freedom.

Women whose potentials are not taken seriously today can and must show their powers. Fundamental change in this regard is not a far-fetched dream and neither is the emancipation of all mankind. The only practical solution for emancipation is born out of a theory that upholds the human being as the most sacred being for humankind and consequently pursues equality as its goal. This is the horizon before us and we shall definitely succeed in reaching it.

2

Fundamentalism and Women

ENTIRELY BASED ON GENDER APARTHEID

In the mindset of Khomeini and his fundamentalist followers, the most important boundary in relationships among human beings is based on gender. Putting aside the historical and fundamental differences in this example, one can claim that just as the ideology and culture of Hitler's fascism was based on racial supremacy, Khomeini-type fundamentalism is based on gender apartheid. If one day, the fundamentalists discard the notion of men's inherent and eternal hegemony over women, they would in effect undergo an essential transformation. They would no longer retain their current identity and would not be able to continue to maintain their present political system. Male-dominance plays a pivotal role in the fundamentalist value system and in their defined standards of piety, charity, sin and punishment, among others. Consequently, they believe that a man is superior and a woman is considered a slave meant to serve him.[1]

---

1. On the eve of the Fourth World Conference of Women in Bejing, the mullahs' Cultural Revoltion Council published a critique of the Convention on the Elimination of All Forms of Discrimination against Women (CEDAW). This is a very telling document about institutionalization of discrimination against women in the mullahs' regime. This document describes CEDAW as "one of the concentrated and grassroot works of the UN" to realize "colonial goals under the mask of defending women's rights". The document states that "the spirit ruling this convention", i.e. equality of men and women, is essentially incompatible with

The founder of this regime, Khomeini, wrote in his book, the *Tahrir al-vasila*: "Women are evil beings. If a woman refuses to create the suitable conditions to please her husband, her husband has a right to beat her up, increasing the intensity of the beating on a daily basis in order to force her into submission."[2]

Fundamentalist theoreticians do not, in their final analysis, regard women as human beings even though the more recent of their thinkers have decided to take a more ambiguous stance on the topic. For example, Mottahari[3] says in contradictory terms that, "Women and men are equal in terms of their humanity, but are two distinct human beings with two different types of characteristics and psychologies... This does not arise out of geographical, historical or social factors, but has been designed in the context of Creation. Nature had certain goals when creating such differences and any action against nature and its constitution would bear undesirable consequences."[4]

Rafsanjani, the mullahs' former President, stressing the "different physical structure and powers" in men and women, has claimed: "Equality has no priority over justice. Justice does not imply that

the foundations of the clerical regime. It further cites Khomeini's remarks to the leaders of the Iranian regime, when he said, "Express abhorrence to the idea of equal rights (for women and men)". The document adds, "According to the Imam (Khomeini) the idea of equality will destroy divine rules in all respects and is oppression against women. The Imam threatened the person who said this with excommunication."

2. Tahrir al-vasila (Instrument of Writing), section on marriage and divorce, nashouz discourse, first question.

3. Ayatollah Morteza Mottahari (1919-1979) was one of Khomeini's senior students. After the fall of the Shah, Khomeini appointed him to head a so-called Revolutionary Council that ran the country's affairs for several months. Prior to the 1979 revolution, Mottahari wrote a number of books in which he tried to present Khomeini's reactionary views wrapped in modern vernacular. He is therefore known as one of the main theoreticians of the fundamentalist regime presently ruling Iran.

4. Morteza Mottahari, Nezam-e Hoqouq-e Zan Dar Eslam (The Rights of Women in Islam), Sadra Publications, Tehran: 1990, p. 18.

all laws should be equal for both women and men... Differences in height, fitness, voice, growth, structure of muscles and physical abilities between men and women indicate that men are stronger and more capable in all these regards... The man's brain is larger; men are more rational and logical while most women are emotional and sentimental... These influence the allocation of responsibilities, duties and rights."[5]

The so-called threat of disregarding physiological differences between women and men is illusive. The real danger, which has had a lasting impact throughout history, is the emphasis placed on these differences to provide the theoretical foundation for gender discrimination. Based on these differences, Mottahari affirms: "Men's spiritual superiority over women has been designed by Mother Nature. It is useless for women to try, however hard, to defy this reality. Since women are more sensitive than men, they must accept the fact that they need men's supervision over their lives."[6]

In this viewpoint, the right to divorce is reserved exclusively for men. According to Mottahari: "If the man decides not to lose his wife and remain loyal to her, then the wife will also love him and remain loyal to him. [Therefore,] nature has placed the natural key to the termination of marriage in the hands of the man."[7]

From this standpoint, the woman gains her self-confidence from the man and does everything she can to earn his trust. Her flesh, soul and identity belong to the man and she identifies herself through the man's identity.

We believe that this sort of thinking is anti-monistic and puts the man in place of God, for a woman. This thinking is against Islam,

5. State-run newspaper, Ettela'at, June 7, 1986

6. Mottahari, op.cit., pp. 215-6.

7. Ibid., p. 267.

because in Islam, the essence of a human being is not defined by physiological differences between the sexes or by racial and ethnic variations, but is rather attributable to the exclusive qualities of humans such as awareness, volition and a sense of responsibility. Accordingly, there are no differences in the duties and responsibilities of a man and a woman.

When the fundamentalists seized power in Iran, the misogynous interpretation of Islam expanded beyond mere theory and was codified into law.

MISOGYNY CODIFIED IN THE LAWS

The constitution of the *Velayat-e Faqih* (the absolute rule of a jurisprudent) predicates gender equality on the "observance of Islamic rules," namely the rulings of the misogynous religion of the mullahs which most violently enforces inequality against women. The laws of the clerical regime deprive women of their rights to be elected as presidents, leaders or judges. The statutes in this regime are also filled with misogyny and gender discrimination.[8]

In the genuine doctrine of Islam, a woman is the owner of all her thoughts and her body. The reactionaries, however, believe that the man owns his wife's body and soul. They see a woman as the slave of a man and justify this way of thinking under the guise of the sanctity of the institution of family.

The Iranian regime's civil code says that the man is the head of the family while the woman must remain dependent on her husband for affairs concerning housing, divorce, employment, nationality, education and travel, among others. The civil code has been written on the basis of discrimination against women and various chapters

---

8. The misogynous laws of the mullahs' regime have been fully explained at the end of this book.

are filled with obvious instances of inequality in the most oppressive forms.

The Islamic Punishment Act, which is the current penal code in Iran, is not only misogynous, but it officially legitimizes violence and torture. The laws drawn up for stoning, for example, are designed to torture the victim in the most vicious way possible.[9]

Stoning is absolutely not condoned by the Quran nor is it in any way related to Islam. It is a legacy of primitive societies and was also formulated in the laws of Talmud and past religions. [10]

Public hanging of a woman, Tehran

---

9. Section 4 of the Act describes the procedures for punishment by stoning to death. Article 104 states, for example, "The stones shall not be so big so as to kill the person by one or two strikes, neither shall the stone be so small that it cannot be called a stone." An English version of the Act is available on <http://www.iranhrdc.org/english/human-rights-documents/iranian-codes/3200-islamic-penal-code-of-the-islamic-republic-of-iran-book-one-and-book-two.html>

10. Will Durant, The Story of Civilization, vol. 1, p. 387 (of the Farsi translation)

A MISOGYNISTIC OUTLOOK

From the standpoint of fundamentalism, sexual sin or piety is the main yardstick by which a value system is measured. The most heinous and unforgivable sins are considered to be sexual lapses. Piety or purity is also judged through a lens of sexual purity and hardly oversteps the individual bounds into the greater political and social domains. Purity and corruption are essentially evaluated and interpreted on the basis of sexual behavior. The socialization of this yardstick has led to the creation of higher walls for dividing the genders. Fundamentalists see women as ominous, evil creatures that symbolize sin and seduction and must not leave the confines of their homes, since their mere presence in society at large would cause others to commit sin.

Meanwhile, at home, the woman must slavishly serve the man's carnal desires so that he would not have to commit sins outside the home. The reactionaries look at both life and the afterlife through their misogynistic spectacles. They have even created myths about the story of Prophet Mohammad's ascension to Heaven (Me'raj) in an attempt to emphasize the importance of avoiding sexual sins. They cite the Prophet as saying, for example: "I saw a woman hanging from her hair whose brain was boiling because she had not covered her hair. I saw a woman who had been hanged from her tongue and hell's boiling water was being poured into her throat, because she had annoyed her husband. I saw a woman hanging from her feet in a furnace of fire, because she had stepped out of home without her husband's permission…"[11]

---

11. Allameh Majlissi, Hayat al-Qoloob ("Life of Hearts"), vol 2, p. 292. Mohammad Baqer Majlissi, known as Allameh Majlissi, lived in the 17th century AC. He was one of the most renowned scholars in religious sciences at the time of the Safavid Dynasty and enjoyed widespread influence in the court of the dynasty's last king. He wrote and compiled many books on the history of Islam and the life and remarks of the leaders of Islam. Considerable parts of his works deal with distorted and altered interpretations attributed to Islam.

Such fabricated myths are nowhere to be found in the Quran. The Quran contains more than 6,200 verses, the great majority of which deal with ontology, history and the nature of humankind while emphasizing human responsibility. The total number of verses focusing on religious precepts does not exceed 500 and only a handful of them deal with sexual vice and virtue.

In the stories narrated from the Prophet, there are seven mortal sins: losing faith in God's mercy, homicide, robbing the belongings of orphans, sorcery and demagoguery, usury, escaping holy war and slandering against women. All these instances of sin relate in one way or another to society at large. So, the question is, "Why do fundamentalists take pains to underscore sexual segregation as a major criterion, while in Islam making accusations against women is a cardinal sin?"

The answer is: They do so because this is the only way they can sit on the throne of religious power and abuse religion in a most despicable manner. They make multitudes of people turn inward while vehemently reproaching them on a religious basis.

On one side are throngs of sinners who must look for a way to compensate for their sins; on the other are the mullahs who portray themselves as clear of all sin and distant from forbidden sexual limits. Through this mechanism, they make the depressed and isolated "sinners" become obedient. "Sinful" individuals are obligated to serve their "pious supreme leader" while believing that the more sins they commit, the more they will have to serve the mullahs.

It thus becomes clear why the fundamentalists put so much emphasis on sexual sins. They do so as a means of creating and maintaining a suppressive social apparatus. Under the domination of men, women are seen as objects for satisfying men's sexual desires and as beings that constantly challenge men's willpower. Men, in contrast to women, are considered to have free will and to be masters of their desires and must prove their worth through suppressing the sources of sin (i.e. women) in a bid to reach the purity promised to them by the mullahs. The mullahs, in turn, impose their own status on society and present themselves as ideal human beings, something that members of society will never attain. The mullahs, both the sources and guardians of an outlook based on sexual drives in the world, impose their will and power, while also acting as this social system's legislators and suppressive forces. Under the rule of the mullahs in Iran, there are dozens of patrols and spying institutions whose main function is to find excuses for furthering this suppression in all commercial offices and other social institutions.

THE DYNAMICS OF SOCIAL SUPPRESSION

One of the important attributes that qualitatively distinguishes the suppressive acts of fundamentalists from those committed by all other forms of dictatorship is interference in the most detailed aspects of people's private lives. In this way, fear permeates deep down in society with justifications in Sharia law about the most hidden aspects of women's behavior.

Under these pretexts, the regime's Revolutionary Guards and the paramilitary Bassij forces raid private parties and launch on-the-spot street inspections, citing a mandate to check and control women and their relations with men on the basis of their self-proclaimed version of Islam.

The mullahs issue directives specifying the color and style of women's attire. They also issue instructions that ban women from such things as laughing in public or participating as spectators in soccer matches. By taking these measures, they boost the morale of their ardent forces while claiming that these measures serve the goals of Islam.[12]

The ticket issued for a woman in Tehran for wearing nail polish: 22,500 rials (roughly $23) for polishing 4.5 fingers.

In the table of fines, the punishments for these types of "crimes" are listed:

Placing glasses over the head: 18,000 rials

Wearing short garbs: 35,000 rials

Wearing brightly colored garbs: 35,000 rials

Wearing nail polish: 5,000 rials for each finger

Bright hair color: 50,000 to 150,000 rials, depending on the color

Now, if misogyny were rejected, the religious structures that grew out of its foundation would be rendered irrelevant. As a result, the mullahs and fundamentalists would no longer have their theoreti-

---

12. In the Iranian regime's Penal Code, the punishment for unveiled women is imprisonment from 10 days to two months. As for improper veiling, which is an undefined charge, there is a list of various punishments.

cal support structure, and what would remain is a normal police or military dictatorship disarmed of all its religious justifications.

The source of all claims made by the mullahs and the source of all the distractions, attractions and positions of the fundamentalists is misogyny. For example, their opposition to Western democracies and their anti-colonialist mottos stem from their assumption that they cause women to step out of the confines of their homes.

Those who have lived in Iran or follow its developments can easily see the truth of the statement that fundamentalists treat the country as if it were occupied. They consider women as spoils of war. They view them as their prisoners and want to have a free hand in committing all forms of violation and abuse against them. On the surface, one hears the mullahs preach about chastity. Behind this deceitful facade, however, are an intention to suppress and the tendency to take possession and commit abuses. This is what victimizes women and has pushed the forces of this regime beyond the limits of humanity.

This basic misogynistic dynamic is the central core around which the regime's suppressive agencies have formed.

When the mullahs seized power in Iran, they encountered a vast energy liberated by the 1979 revolution as well as the prevalence of a powerful tendency in society to overturn obsolete relationships. They used gender apartheid and misogyny to suppress and restrain these enormous energies and potentials.

The mullahs' strengthened the malevolent tendencies of their operatives through the institution of gender segregation and by taking ownership of women, thus creating a force for general suppression.

Systematic sexual discrimination accompanied by physical and psychological oppression degrades and humiliates women. Its practical outcome is increased rates of depression in women in Iran with an unprecedented number of them committing suicide.[13]

The mullahs justify their misogyny and suppression of women by resorting to ethical and religious pretexts. The great contradiction, however, is that prostitution has increased in Iran under the mullahs' rule more than at any other period in Iran's history. Many foreign reporters visiting Iran have said that they were astonished by the high rate of prostitution there.

Indeed, the Iranian regime has itself acknowledged that the age of prostitution has dropped to 13 years, and is prevalent among female school students. State-sponsored gangs are involved in the business of sexual slavery, one of the most profitable businesses in today's Iran. In the aftermath of the earthquake that shook the city of Bam in the winter of 2004, it was common practice for orphaned girls to be kidnapped. This was pointed out in reports by foreign teams who had traveled to Bam to provide humanitarian aid to the quake victims.

SUPPRESSION OF WOMEN, THE MAIN EXPRESSION OF FUNDAMENTALISM

People around the world have been exposed to only an insignificant portion of the real tragedy that has gripped the lives of women in my homeland.

The mullahs' regime has descended with colossal destruction on all the rights and freedoms, as well as the culture, family and private lives, of Iranian women:

---

13. Iran is the third country in the world where the growing rate of women's suicide is predicted to take over that of men. The first and second ranks belong to China and India. In all countries, the number of men who die after committing suicide is three times the number of women killed in the same manner... In Iran, however, research shows that the number of women attempting suicide is three times that of men. (Deutsche Welle Radio, September 9, 2007)

- Thousands of dissident women have been executed, a statistic that is unprecedented in the world;

- Tens of thousands of women have been tortured as political prisoners;

- Pregnant women have been executed, and mothers tortured in front of their children;

- Women's social and economic statuses have been diminished, turning them into second-class citizens;

- Gender apartheid has been instituted in society;

- Women's regular movement in the streets is under constant scrutiny;

- Veiling has become compulsory, with additional controls over the type and color of women's attire, while women's faces have been cut with blades or burnt with acid for violating the dress code;

- Women have been deprived of the right to divorce and cannot have custody of their own children;

- Distorted forms of marriage, including polygamy and temporary marriages, have become prevalent and justified in various ways by the mullahs' abysmal ideology;

- Medieval and draconian punishments such as stoning, whose victims are primarily women, have been instituted;

- There is injustice and discrimination in economic cooperation, employment and education;

- Young girls —whose families are forced to sell them out of poverty and destitution in a country as rich as Iran —are being trafficked to foreign countries by criminal factions of the clerical regime;

- Body parts of innocent, starving and impoverished girls are being sold;

There is systematic rape of women in prisons.[14]

Rape is the main form of torturing women in the mullahs' dungeons and other suppressive organs. When all forms of torture and even execution and massacre fail to discourage women from entering the field of struggle, and when torturers fail to break the celebrated determination of the female Mojahedin and activists to wage resistance, the mullahs and their Revolutionary Guards employ the last form of leverage at their disposal: rape, sexual slander and degradation. The most detested torturers in the history of the cleri-

---

14. In summer 2009, presidential hopeful Mehdi Karroubi, the Parliament Speaker for two terms, revealed that revolutionary guards and prison guards raped incarcerated men and women. In a letter on July 29, 2009 to Ali Akbar Hashemi Rafsanjani, then-Head of the Assembly of Experts, Karroubi wrote, "A number of those arrested have mentioned that some people rape impriosoned girls so viciously that their genitals are torn and injured. Furthermore, imprisoned boys are also savagely raped. Some of them have consequently become depressed, suffer from serious psychological and physical disorders and hide at home… The people who told me this hold sensitive positions in this country, renowned authorities, a number of whom served in the Sacred War."

Karroubi submitted specific documents and evidence regarding these claims. Predictably, however, the clerical regime's judiciary rejected the case.

The Times of London wrote on September 18, 2009,

"The Times has been given access to 500 pages of documents — a small fraction of the total — that include handwritten testimony by victims, medical reports and interviews.

'Reports of the use of rape and torture were similar across prisons in Tehran and in other provinces,' wrote one investigator.

"The documents also suggest that a chain of unofficial, makeshift prisons has been set up across Iran where rape and torture are common practice. In Tehran alone, 37 young men and women claim to have been raped by their jailers. Doctors' reports say that two males, aged 17 and 22, died as a result of severe internal bleeding after being raped… Many of the male rape victims also spoke of beatings, being subjected to forms of sexual humiliation, including riding naked colleagues, and living in their underwear in filthy conditions."

In the 1980s, a large number of young opponents of the Iranian regime, including thousands of young girls, were detained in political prisons. Khomeini issued a decree sanctioning the rape of young girls who had been condemned to death. The decree was religiously justified to deprive virgin girls from going to Heaven after execution. So, the revolutionary guards were duty-bound to rape them before execution. The practice of rape against female prisoners has been a systematic form of torture practiced in Iranian jails ever since.

cal regime's prisons, such as Assadollah Lajevardi and Haj Davoud Rahmani, are infamous for committing rape. In the 1980s, women's prisons included a unit called the residential unit, which existed as a place for raping female prisoners. Female prisoners were told, "We will do things to you which would prevent you from having the courage to return to your families."[15]

"Rape" is also the *raison d'être* of the clerical regime's Vice Bureaus.[16] The savagery committed to date against defenseless women and girls in these places forms a voluminous case.

---

15. The Residential Unit was an apartment complex belonging to the prison's personnel that was turned into a special ward of the women's prison in the early 1980s. In this ward, the revolutionary guards and torturers were absolutely free to commit wicked crimes against women. The ward is infamous among revolutionary guards as "haram" and the prisoners taken there are considered "booty." A former political prisoner who spent several years in prison, said: "Our information about the Residential Unit is very limited because hardly anyone who returned from the Residential Unit was of sound mind. Everyone returning from the Residential Unit suffered from some form of severe mental disorder. They either did not tell us anything or did not remember anything at all about what had been done to them." Another prisoner wrote: "The things we know about the Residential Unit are limited to the scattered, sometimes irrelevant and incoherent statements by the insane." Another wrote, "After months, I managed to build a relation with one of the returnees of the Residential Unit and gain her trust. She told me that they had been forced to eat at the same table with their interrogators and torturers. This is very distressful for a prisoner, especially when you are a woman. Then, with the slightest excuse, like beginning to eat without the permission of your interrogator, they beat the prisoner with cables, flogs or anything else, so much that she went unconscious. Then the prisoner was forced to say, 'I was wrong.' Then they had to kiss the hand of the interrogator before they could begin to eat their food. Again, there would be another excuse. The prisoner had to place the interrogator's food in the plate and offer it to him and if she refused, the same scene would repeat. Whenever we began to get close to the topic of sexual assaults in the Residential Unit, this prisoner became so hysterical, that she could not continue." Another prisoner wrote: "In this unit, prisoners were kept on foot for several consecutive days and not allowed to rest. They were forced to run in the yard under snow and in cold weather. They were forced to make animal noises. This was done simultaneously with the tapes of clerics singing sermons being loudly broadcast from loudspeakers in the unit. The pressure was so great that it made many prisoners decide to commit suicide."

16. The agency promoting virtue and fobidding vice, also known as the Vice Bureau, was formed to control the interaction among the population, particularly those between men and women. Raiding private parties and arresting the guests, on-the-spot interrogation of boys and girls in the streets, controlling women's make-up and dress by issuing fines and making arrests

In February 2004, after returning from a weeklong visit to Tehran, Dr. Yakin Erturk, then-the UN Human Rights Commission Special Rapporteur on Violence against Women , reported that Iranian women had been condemned to death on the basis of false evidence. In many instances, the case was turned against the woman who filed the complaint in the first place. Even victims of rape faced numerous obstacles before being heard.

This is why we continue to maintain that this regime is at war with the people of Iran. This is why the Iranian people's democratic struggle against this regime is not limited to the regime's uranium enrichment, nuclear program or even its relationship with Iraq. Their struggle is against the entirety of religious fascism, whose culture and history can be summed up by rape and assault: Rape and assault of the dignity, respect and rights of Iranian women and men.

Therefore, women across Iran should know that although the pain of inequality, humiliation and disrespect has filled their hearts and although the mullahs have trampled upon their personal, familial, social and political rights and opted to destroy their human identity, there is a potential in them that has turned Iranian women into forces capable of toppling the mullahs' regime.

Iranian women shake the foundations of the mullahs' rule when they rise up in the heart of Tehran and chant that freedom and a minimum wage are the indisputable rights of the people of Iran. Their determination will help realize the demands of the people of Iran. They are Iran's future.

The clerical regime's animosity towards and crimes against women stem from the fact that they are terrified of them. Iranian society is filled with new demands and a burning desire for change. The com-

---

are among the duties of this suppressive organ. The agents of this bureau have arrested numerous women and girls for "behavior contardicting purity" or for "improper veiling," and subsequently raped them in their detention centers.

33

pressed energy for change in Iran resides in women as the pioneers of this struggle. They are the ones that can definitively defeat the fundamentalists.

SPREADING MISOGYNY TO OTHER COUNTRIES

Fundamentalism, due to its very nature, cannot be limited to the confines of geographical borders. When spilling over to other countries, fundamentalism spreads its misogyny as well. The expansion of fundamentalism and misogyny can be studied from three different angles:

First, the export and expansion of Islamic fundamentalism is dependent on the rule of fundamentalists in Iran. The Iranian regime has never concealed its strategic goal of establishing a global Islamic empire. Mohammad Khatami, a former president of the regime, has said, "In the strategy of preserving the Islamic Revolution, we must have in mind 'expansion' and not mere 'preservation'."[17] Second, Islamic fundamentalism is not compatible with modernity. It, therefore, seeks to survive under any circumstance by attacking and expanding into other countries. This is why Khomeini insisted on continuing eight years of war with Iraq, often saying, "War is the basis of life," and "Peace would mean the burial of Islam."

The third aspect of examining the spread of fundamentalism is the existence of suitable conditions for its growth in recent decades. Two very important factors in this regard are the disintegration of the former Soviet Union and the decline of Arab nationalism due to the Gulf War.

In 1988, when the first signs of instability emerged in the Soviet Union, Khomeini wrote a letter to the Soviet leader Mikhail

---

17. Khatami was explaining the doctrine of the "export of revolution" in a roundtable discussion on the "National Security Strategy of the Islamic Republic of Iran." His comments were published in Resalat newspaper on July 7, 1991.

Gorbachev inviting him to convert to Islam! Although this seemed to be a diplomatically frivolous measure, it demonstrated the mullahs' intent in advancing their fundamentalist objectives.[18]

In the early 1990s, the Iranian resistance underscored that "Islamic fundamentalism" was "the new global threat."[19] Unfortunately, few people took it seriously back then, but with the passing of time and after witnessing bitter catastrophes like the one on September 11, 2001, the situations in Afghanistan and Iraq and the situation of Muslims in Western countries, the accuracy of the Iranian resistance's assessment was confirmed and validated.[20]

Amid the uproar of the mullahs' warmongering and terrorism in the Middle East and Islamic countries, the trampling of women's rights and freedoms has not been very evident. But, in fact, fundamentalism has thrown the lives of women in these countries backwards to a point in the distant past.

---

18. This letter was issued on January 1, 1989.

19. *Islamic Fundamentalism: The New Global Threat* was published by the Foreign Relations Committee of the National Council of Resistance of Iran in 1993, offering an in-depth study of the historical precedence of *Velayat-e Faqih*, its reactionary nature and its instruments of survival, i.e. domestic repression and exportation of terrorism. The book analyzed the phenomenon of Islamic Fundamentalism that was, until then, unknown to the world and explained its danger to Muslim societies and peace in the Middle East. The book suggested that the solution to Islamic fundamentalism would be a democratic Islam. See Mohammad Mohaddessin, *Islamic Fundamentalism: The New Global Threat*, Seven Locks Press, 1993.

20. In 1994, on the invitation of Norwegian parties, Maryam Rajavi travelled to Norway where she warned against the danger of the leviathan of religious tyranny and Islamic fundamentalism whose heart beats in Tehran. At the time, seven years before the September 11 attacks, while the West remained ignorant of this growing threat and overlooked the Iranian regime's obvious role in terrorist attacks including the one on the Khobar Towers in Saudi Arabia, Mrs. Rajavi said, "Islamic fundamentalism has become the most dangerous threat to the world and to peace in the Middle East... Iran's ruling mullahs abuse the religious beliefs of over a billion Muslims to expand their rule, export crisis and build tension. Interfering in the affairs of Islamic countries, issuing death decrees for foreign nationals, terrorist operations in various countries, allocating delirious budgets for procurement of various types of weapons including weapons of mass destruction (biological and chemical) and especially efforts to gain nuclear arms, are only part of their behavior and positions on the international scene. Such manners are entwined with the nature and existence of these reactionaries."

Among other countries, Iraq has always been the prime target for the mullahs' exportation of fundamentalism. Its unique geopolitical features such as its majority Shiite population, its status as the host of the tombs of six Shiite imams, and the fact that it shares a 1,200 kilometer-long border with Iran, make Iraq a ripe fruit, as the mullahs say, ready to be harvested.

Although the Iranian resistance was the first to expose the clerical regime's nuclear program and weapons of mass destruction, today the growing danger of Tehran's meddling in Iraq is a hundred times greater than the regime's nuclear menace. The clerical regime works to export fundamentalism to Iraq by dispatching its agents who have been trained in Qom and Tehran. Women are the first victims of this advance of fundamentalism into Iraq.

Forty-five years ago, Iraqi women had gained some rights after the adoption of a new family law called, "The Law on Personal Status." Those rights included prohibiting arbitrary divorce by men, allowing divorced mothers to take custody of their children and restricting polygamy.

After 2003, however, when the U.S. attacked Iraq and made the greater mistake of allowing Tehran-backed groups to rule Iraq, the country's women's rights and freedoms began to degenerate and were replaced by an ever-expanding gender apartheid system. They practically lost many of the rights that they had previously enjoyed and were condemned to live in fear, insecurity and poverty.

It is chilling to hear that attacking, killing and raping women is rampant in the neighboring country of Iraq. Female doctors and professors are assassinated and girls are kidnapped from the streets; incidents like the raping of female university students by paramilitary troops are ongoing. Beauty salons are attacked and destroyed. A large number of female students in high schools and universities have been forced to drop out of school. Some schools for girls have even been closed down, resulting in a large number of women becoming poor and homeless.

The fundamentalist threat against women's rights and liberties has also increased drastically in other countries like Afghanistan, Pakistan, Lebanon, Palestine, Algeria, Sudan and Somalia. A number of countries have imitated the misogynous laws established by Iran's clerical rulers. Punishment by stoning has emerged in other countries after it was carried out by the regime in Iran. Compulsory veiling and depriving women of the freedom to choose the way they dress have also been exported from Iran to many Muslim countries.

FUNDAMENTALISTS IN WESTERN COUNTRIES

In Western countries, fundamentalists wish to create a bogus confrontation between Islamic and Western cultures. The issue of women is the most serious topic in this cultural challenge. Reports on the situation of Muslim women in these countries are shocking.

Two decades ago, it was inconceivable to hear of a woman rejecting examination by a male doctor, especially if her life depended on it. Today, however, we face such occurrences.

This happens despite the fact that the simple, unraveling principle in the authentic Islamic canon stresses *Yosr*, which means ease and simplicity. The Quran clearly emphasizes that those in poor health are not obliged to participate in fasting. On the same grounds, it is not permissible to put one's life at risk because the doctor is male or female. Therefore, during times of serious illness or a threat to one's life, examination by any doctor (be it male or female) is permitted without any hindrances.

The fact is that today's Muslim women seek refuge in reactionary and fundamentalist ideologies as a response to the degradation of women in Western culture because they cannot see an acceptable alternative.

3

Democratic Islam, The Ideological and Political Response to Fundamentalism

IN SEARCH OF AN ENLIGHTENED ISLAM

While Islamic fundamentalism has become a global threat, we must figure out how it can be best remedied. It is evident that one should look for an effective ideological and political response in the face of such a threat. If we do so, we will clearly discover that the answer lies in a "democratic Islam," since no one can ask more than 750 million Muslim women or 1.5 billion total Muslims worldwide to reject fundamentalism in favor of a non-Islamic model. While the central element in this response is Islam itself, it is a genuine Islam that is democratic and stands as the antithesis to fundamentalism.

The immediate question then is, "What is the truth of Islam?" Is it what the fundamentalist rulers of Iran claim it to be? Are the crimes committed by the clerical regime in Iran under the banner of Islam truly rooted in Islam?

The fact is that the mullahs have nothing to do with genuine Islam. It would be the greatest gift to the mullahs to regard their actions as Islamic. The worst deceit of our time is that reactionary charlatans like Khomeini have portrayed themselves as symbols of Islam. On the other hand, Islam should be viewed as the religion of hope, compassion, emancipation, freedom, love, friendship, peace, progress, tolerance, lenience, kindness, clemency and selflessness to promote comfort and freedom for others. It is a religion that embodies all the beauties of the earth and all the genuine beauties and values that characterize humanity. Islam has the greatest respect for human beings, especially women, and seeks equality and freedom for them. Meanwhile, the reactionary mullahs preach that Islam is a religion of hardships, torture, revenge, war, misery, despair, spite, coercion, compulsion and all the darkness and evil on earth; in a word, a religion that buries humanity alive.

The mullahs should be asked: "Where in Islam have the crimes you commit been endorsed? Where in Islam and the Quran have the killing and massacre of political prisoners, especially thousands of women including 13-year-old girls, 70-year-old mothers and pregnant women, endorsed? Where does Islam say you are permitted to label women, humiliate them on the streets, stone them or rape and harass them in prison torture chambers? Is it not the explicit guidance of the Quran that there is to be no compulsion in religion?"

Fundamentalists overemphasize the *hijab* (veiling) and other similar issues on the basis of gender segregation, offering a distorted picture of the religion, as if Islam is exclusively concerned about such issues. A quick glance at the Quran, however, shows that out of a total of 6,234 verses, only three or four reference the *hijab*. Here, you can see the charlatanism of the mullahs in drawing up a picture of Islam that is all about the *hijab*. [1]

---

1. Only a month after the mullahs seized power in Iran, Khomeini's operatives attacked women on the streets with the slogan of "either the veil or a hit on the head." This was to lay the grounds for imposing compulsory *hijab* (veiling) on women. The PMOI officially denounced such suppressive behavior and forcible veiling. PMOI women's role was significant in those days in confronting this phenomenon. Although they wore scarves, they bravely stood up against the detested slogan of "either the veil or a hit on the head." Even before the fall of the Shah and the 1979 revolution, PMOI women resisted the mullahs' misogyny, which was gradually emerging in those days while the mullahs were still in the opposition. *Kayhan* daily, January 17, 1979, no. 10615, wrote on page 7: "PMOI women published a revealing statement denouncing

Against this medieval regime, the experience of the Iranian resistance movement is living proof of Islam's conviction to equality. The pioneering women of the Iranian resistance who have undertaken the most crucial responsibilities in the liberation movement have been inspired by a democratic Islam that believes in equality. They have been able to lead a movement in the face of an overzealous religious dictatorship. They have been able to overcome the myths about women's weaknesses. They have not only freed women but also men from the shackles of exploitation. They have been able to pave the path for defeating Iran's ruling fundamentalists.

This experience is accompanied by numerous achievements, all of which could be summarized in an effective response to fundamentalism that lies in a democratic Islam.

The philosophical foundations and theoretical bases of the PMOI's democratic Islam were drawn up by Mohammad Hanifnejad and Massoud Rajavi years before Khomeini took power. This outlook stood diametrically opposed to the reactionary and feudalist interpretations of Islam by Khomeini and others, and was based on the Quran and authentic Islamic texts. The Mojahedin's democratic Islam was embraced by millions of young intellectuals and students in Iran and endorsed by great scholars like Ayatollah Mahmoud Taleqani.[2]

---

the uncouth acts of a small number of people who threaten unveiled women and girls with burning, stabbing and acid throwing. These actions, caused by lack of knowledge and incited by treacherous propaganda of mercenary elements, toll the alarm bells."

2. Ayatollah Seyyed Mahmoud Taleqani was a popular and highly respected religious leader in Iran. He was a bitter opponent of religious fundamentalism, and a highly regarded interpreter and scholar of Quran. He was also a key figure in the anti-monarchic revolution of 1979, and began defending the rights of the Iranian people in the 1930s. During the reign of the Mohammad-Reza Shah, he was arrested and tortured on several occasions. After the fall of the Shah in 1979, Taleqani became an outspoken critic of the fundamentalists led by Khomeini who were trying to monopolize political power. He famously described "dictatorship under the cloak of religion" as the worst kind of tyranny. He died in September 1979 at the age of 68..

In the field of practice and throughout the years of confrontation between democratic Islam and Khomeini's fundamentalism (from 1979 to now), the quarrel has always been over freedom. While Khomeini trampled upon all his promises about freedoms after he seized power, the PMOI stressed from the very early days that the main question in the Iranian revolution is the question of "fundamental freedoms."

A few months later, in the summer of 1979, Khomeini raised the issue of "*Velayat-e Faqih,*" which was vehemently rejected by the Mojahedin. The PMOI subsequently boycotted the referendum on the constitution of Khomeini's *Velayat-e Faqih* regime.

In 1981, when Khomeini wanted to have the retribution bill passed by the *Majlis* (parliament), the PMOI not only called it anti-Islamic, but also denounced it as "inhumane."

In the years that followed, the feud between these two forces over Islam continued, each side having completely differing philosophical, cultural, historical and political standards. The feud over freedom between democratic and fundamentalist interpretations of Islam has naturally led to two profoundly different outlooks on women and their rights and freedoms; just like today where the issue of democracy in any society is intertwined with the issue of equality.

What distinguishes democratic Islam from other fundamentalist and reactionary interpretations is their approach to the question of women.

Today, the debate revolves around which of these two interpretations is right about Islamic philosophy and truth, with each side claiming to be the followers of the true Islam. What can provide clarity and outline the differences between these two sides is the way each camp answers the following question: Does Islam, at its core, really harbor misogyny?

DYNAMISM OF THE QURAN

The reactionaries argue that Islamic laws and edicts must be enforced today exactly as they were 1,400 years ago. Perhaps this is why they are referred to as fundamentalists. Of course, they dogmatically adhere to minor commandments and outdated forms while sacrificing the principles and fundamentals for their own petty interests. In the 20th century, they absurdly calculated religious fines and tithes based on the worth of camels, sheep, dates and coins that were in circulation 14 centuries ago.

The Quran is the most sacred book of Islam. Although it is not primarily a book of laws, parts of its verses nonetheless prescribe rules to be applied in economic and social spheres. Of course, these verses cover only a limited portion of the Quran, and they do not reflect all the rules and precepts.

Among the verses containing rules, for example, there are a few referring to the laws of inheritance, indicating that a woman's share is half that of a man. Another verse indicates that a testimony made by two women is equal to a testimony made by one man. Other verses do not include specific rules but contain phrases that appear discriminatory and run counter to women's rights.

One may wonder how one can believe that Islam is compatible with the notion and values of equality while the text of these verses cannot be changed or removed from the Quran. And, does this not lead to the definitive conclusion that the rules in the Quran and Islam are fixed and unalterable, making it unrealistic to attribute the notion of equality to Islam?

Beyond the precepts and the historical rules, one must strive to grasp the spirit of Islam and the Quran's genuine outlook. The precepts must not be considered as unalterable dogmas. Rather, as circumstances change, they must be replaced by newer precepts that better comply with Islam's social ideals. This is called the dynamism of the Quran. With such dynamism, it is able to answer the problems and needs of humanity and society over time. If such dynamism is overlooked, reactionary thought, oppression and discrimination would ultimately emerge under the guise of Islam.

Resorting to a dogmatic and formalistic outlook while disregarding substance and spirit is not limited to thinking about Islam and has a long history. To distinguish right from wrong, one must first differentiate between the strategic goals and the tactical means for reaching those goals. Consider, for example, a boat sailing towards the shore. The ultimate goal is to reach the shore and the strategy is to sail in a straight, fixed course towards land. The acts of paddling, adjusting speed and other considerations at varying stages in the journey should never be considered as fixed or inflexible. Otherwise, tactics will take the place of strategy and divert or reverse the initial course. As a result, the actual goal would be forgotten and replaced by the means.

Thus, it is imperative that we move towards the main goal without being bogged down by dogmatic thought and, at the same time, steer clear of opportunism and self-serving actions (i.e. being injudicious about the time-dependent rules and laws). If we fail to do so, we would certainly steer off the main path.

To understand the true spirit of the Quran, let us refer to it directly, while noting that it rejects all forms of reactionary and antiquated interpretations of it and Islam as a whole. The Quran divides and characterizes verses as follows: Some are unambiguous and firm (*muhkamat*), they form the foundation of the book; others are allegorical or ambiguous (*mutashabihat*). But people with ill hearts use the allegorical verses as a pretext for their interpretations and sow the seeds of discord.[3]

The *muhkamat* are verses forming the ideological foundations of Islam. They include the philosophical, ontological and anthropological content and bases of Islam. *Mutashabihat*, however, are verses dealing with rules of day-to-day life and are not fixed in any way. Rather, they can be revised and reformed, on the basis of the same monotheistic substance, in order to pave the way for the advancement of humankind and the fulfillment of social requirements at various times. Otherwise, they would be reduced to rigid and useless dogma.

Islam has a dynamism through which it can facilitate social development and progress. Since it does not want to advance this cause through abstract means, Islam's method from the outset has been to demarcate *muhkamat* and *motashabihat*.

In verse 7 of the Family of Imran, the act of conflating fundamental principles with tactical rules is condemned. It warns that relying on allegorical verses is like a whirlwind that drowns those with ill hearts, but that those with knowledge of the spirit of the religion will remain immune from this fate. The guiding principle for the knowledgeable is that the teachings and the message of Islam must be examined holistically in order to differentiate between the unchanging principles or *muhkamat* and the allegorical verses.

Fundamentalists regard historical tactical rules and judgments as dogma and as being unalterable. This approach contradicts the

---

3. Family of Imran, verse 7: He it is Who has sent down to thee the Book: In it are verses basic or fundamental (of established meaning); they are the foundation of the Book: others are allegorical. But those in whose hearts is perversity follow the part thereof that is allegorical, seeking discord, and searching for its hidden meanings, but no one knows its hidden meanings except Allah. And those who are firmly grounded in knowledge say: "We believe in the Book; the whole of it is from our Lord:" and none will grasp the Message except men of understanding.

Quran's definition and classification of verses. As fundamental principles of Islam, *muhkamat* are unalterable while *mutashabihat* are relative, dynamic and flexible. In other places, the Quran uses the term *mathani*, meaning lenient, flexible and dynamic, to describe *mutashabihat*.[4]

Based on their religious dogmatism and reactionary interpretation of Islam, the fundamentalists deliberately predicate idealistic values on practical tactics, which, in the history of Islam, were designed within the historical limits and potentials of that era.

For example, monotheistic values such as respecting women's equality could not have been enforced because the backward realities of society in that era prevented its institution. So, in order to realize the ideals of Islam, periods of transition were essential. Such transient and temporary solutions can be likened to the bottom steps of a ladder on which one has to step before reaching the top. The bottom steps were not symbolic of Islam's ultimate ideals. Nevertheless, the reactionaries consider these transient solutions as the principal values of Islam.

The process of perverting the spirit of Islam gradually entered a more complicated stage. Rulings like the difference in women's share of inheritance, or the conditional grace period considered in some cases for polygamy, have been exploited by reactionaries as a means to craft new interpretations and present their own inventions under the banner of Islam. Accordingly, they propagated the theory of one man being equal to two women as an underlying principle. To further explain this, let us look at several examples.

---

4. The Throngs, verse 23: "Allah has revealed (from time to time) the most beautiful Message in the form of a Book, consistent with itself, (yet) repeating (its teaching in various aspects)..."

INHERITANCE

At the time of its advent 14 centuries ago, Islam set a woman's share of inheritance as half that of a man's. Considering the dynamism of the Quran and the fact that the ruling on women's share of inheritance is an allegorical one, while also recalling the fundamental verse on the equality of men and women, this rule can be altered in accordance with changing socioeconomic conditions.

If we fail to take note of the historical necessities of the time and consider the inheritance rule as fixed and permanent, then we also fail to understand its significance when it was initially prescribed 14 centuries ago. Moreover, we will also falsely conclude that Islam is opposed to women's equality in general. This is certainly not the case, as Islam granted inheritance rights to women who were, at the time, entirely excluded from it and even subjects of inheritance themselves. Because they were considered a possession of their husbands, women were passed down to relatives and members of their husbands' tribe as property. Thus, granting women the right to have a share in inheritance was itself revolutionary. It is absolutely subjective and unrealistic to expect Islam to have declared and enforced full and complete equality for women in those days. We know that it was not until very recently that women enjoyed full financial independence, even in European countries.

The other important point to take note of regarding women's share of inheritance 14 centuries ago is that they did not play any role in the means of production; it was the man's responsibility to provide financially for the family. In light of these facts, it is evident that the Quran's dynamism calls for equal shares of inheritance for men and women whenever socioeconomic progress calls for it and whenever the socioeconomic status of women changes or there is an opportunity for it to change. Because the social conditions and the social and economic roles of men and women in modern times have undergone enormous transformations, the Quran's dynamism would reject men's dominating role and would prescribe gender equality.

TESTIMONY

On the issue of women's competence to exercise correct judgment and assume leadership positions, one must note that the verses in the Quran that order followers to respect justice are addressed to *all* believers. They do not make distinctions based on gender (See, for example, Surah Nisa, Verse 58). God invites all to be honest and exercise justice in their judgments. There is no religious text or fixed tradition that contradicts the Quran by denying a particular section of the population or women the right to sovereignty and judgment.

In verse 282 of Surah Baqarah, there is a reference to the testimony that two women, as opposed to one man, make regarding issues of financial affairs like borrowing and debt. This mention of female testimony is not stated elsewhere in the Quran where testimony by men and women are referenced.

The aforementioned verse explains the reason why two women, rather than one man, should give testimony in such matters and rejects making a generalization out of this rule. The verse explains that the reason why two women should testify is "that if one of them errs, the other can correct her." So if an inability to recall events correctly were of no concern , the second woman's help would not be necessary. Like inhabitants of remote villages in the modern era, women at that time were not able to identify and differentiate between different bills and coins and thus could not count money. Such historic backwardness has caused people to avoid considering women as legitimate witnesses when it came to financial disputes. This verse, however, aims to teach Muslims how to file evidence and refer to witnesses.

In order to prevent the exclusion of women from such spheres, the Quran offers a transient solution to help relieve some of these concerns and provides for the gradual engagement of women in financial matters. A dogmatic approach to this type of testimony, on the other hand, assumes that this rule is fixed and eternal. Furthermore, it concludes the inequality of women and men and attributes this way of thinking to Islam itself. The fact, however, is that in the primitive societies of 14 centuries ago, women did not enjoy any rights and newborn girls were oftentimes buried alive. By offering rules such as the one referencing the testimony of two women, Islam took extremely bold steps in the restitution of women's rights. Now one can begin to see how reactionaries distort Islam's emancipating ideals, messages and rules through their dogmatic interpretations, reducing them to fit their deficient, narrow and commerce-driven minds.

SLAVERY

Another example of the Quran's dynamism is demonstrated through its view on slavery. By taking a closer look at the issue of slavery, a great contradiction in the fundamentalist outlook is revealed.

Because of its dedication to equality and rejection of discrimination, Islam is and has always been fundamentally opposed to slavery. The abolition of slavery, however, was a necessaryhistorical and social bedrock. Today, we know full well that, given the economic conditions of the time and the rudimentary means of production, any calls for the complete abolition of slavery would neither have made progress nor advanced the state of production. Such a premature step would have delayed the complete eradication of slavery. For this reason, it would have been impossible for the Prophet of Islam to instantaneously enforce such ideals in the primitive society of his time by abolishing slavery. Instead, he formulated traditions that led the way towards the elimination of slavery. For example, he announced that many sins could be forgiven if one were to free slaves. This set of rules, which is referred to as the rules and rights of *etq*, implies that the Quran views slavery as tantamount to committing those sins.

In chapters The Cow and The City, the Quran reveres believing slaves more than non-believing reactionaries. Balal Habashi, a black slave, was the spokesman of the Prophet and called people to prayer (*muezzin*).

So, it was the spirit of the judgments and conduct of the Prophet himself that reoriented society towards the abolition of slavery. Otherwise, there were no explicit orders in the Quran for doing so. Nevertheless, the fundamentalists cannot claim today that Islam allows slavery simply because the Quran does not reference its abolition directly or explicitly. Thus, since they cannot portray Islam as a defender of slavery, how can they portray it as a religion that condones women's inequality?

The fundamentalists claim to carry out religious precepts in accordance with the Prophet's conduct. However, this is a blatant deception because it is common knowledge that one of the most brilliant aspects of the Prophet's mission was to emancipate and teach respect for women. It was he who made it a mortal sin to slander a woman and levied a heavy punishment for doing so. He said that to prove such charges, one had to produce four witnesses. Even when faced with a confession of sexual promiscuity, time and again he simply looked the other way and urged the sinner to repent.

The misogynous mullahs, however, slander hundreds of women every day, and arrest and flog or stone them in public. To this, Imam Ali says, "A time will come when nothing will remain of the Quran except its writing and nothing of Islam except its name."[5]

It is worth pointing out here Imam Ali's views on the Quran and its rules. He says, "The Quran has spelled out what is lawful (*halaal*) and unlawful (*haraam*); what is obligatory (*wajeb*) and recommend-

---

5. *Nahj-ol Balagha (The Road to Eloquence)*, edited by Yasin T. Al-Jibouri, saying 379.

ed (*mostahab*); what is renewing (*nassekh*) and outdated (*mansookh*); what is general and specific; what is fundamental (*muhkam*) and allegorical (*mutashabeh*)... Some affairs have been proclaimed obligatory in the Quran while their obligation has been annulled by the Prophet's tradition. There are also certain matters in the Prophet's tradition that have been considered as obligatory while the Quran allows their annulment. There are also matters that were obligatory in their own time, but were later abolished."

Do these explicit remarks by Imam Ali confirm the fundamentalist interpretation or prove the dynamism of the Quran?

The history of Islamic precepts, including those involving prayer, fasting, pilgrimage and other forms of worship, as well as those regarding broader economic and social affairs, is characterized by a trend of progressive transformation. Examining such a trend vis-à-vis these fundamental principles helps us realize the extent of the progress towards the ideals of Islam. We can see an evolution in all the teachings and precepts of Islam, each of which leads us to appreciate the dynamism of Islam and the Quran.

The conclusion that has been drawn is that a dynamic interpretation of Islam is a natural partner for humankind's struggle for freedom and justice and also for the women's equality movement.

Although this outlook is no doubt respected by all freedom-loving and progressive people around the world, one question remains: Is this dynamic interpretation rooted in genuine Islam, or does it stem from a desire to "revise" or "reform" the religion?

The answer is that this interpretation is indeed grounded in the true nature of Islam. This is so because it draws directly from the Quran and the traditions and teachings promulgated by the Prophet Mohammad. It is not tainted by misogyny or colored by the distortions and abuses carried out by oppressive rulers and reactionaries.

Furthermore, this outlook has remained impervious to the interests of male-dominated regimes over the past 14 centuries.

Although we call it democratic Islam, it is most certainly not a new religion, as some will claim. Once we liberate Islam from such tainted views, a colossal revolution (far beyond any reform) will take shape for the future of Muslims and especially for women, who will be filled with a remarkable potential to brush past fundamentalism.

The real history of Islam, its texts and, most importantly, the letter of the Quran all promote justice in general and women's equality in particular.

4

Women's Equality in Islam

ISLAM'S ATTEMPTS TO PAVE THE WAY FOR WOMEN'S EQUALITY

As will be seen later, an evaluation of Islam's attempts to lay the groundwork for women's equality in the context of the socioeconomic conditions of the 7th century leads to the conclusion that no other social revolution has ever transformed women's rights to the same extent with respect to the economic and social circumstances of the time.

If we take into account the socioeconomic conditions prevalent at the time of the advent of Islam in the Arabian Peninsula (whether we have a positive or negative view on Islam), we will realize that it emerged as a religion and a movement in defiance of idolatry among indigenous Arab tribes, and proclaimed the creed of monotheism. At the same time, it publicly set out to address the dismal fate of women and exposed it from the outset. In other words, it is an indisputable fact that the messages and teachings of Islam reprimand misogyny alongside idolatry, tribal wars, poverty, backwardness, etc.

At the time and in the society where the Prophet of Islam received his mission, having a daughter was considered an unfortunate occurrence. The negative social regard towards women at the time was

53

reprimanded by the Quran, as exemplified by the disdain with which it describes men filled with anger upon the birth of a daughter.

In those times, it was a common practice for Arabs to bury newborn girls alive because of the stigma associated with having a daughter. They feared their daughters would be taken as prisoners and enslaved in the course of tribal wars and forced into prostitution. The impoverished portions of the population also worried about caring for them or providing them with the necessary dowry for marriage. The Quran addresses this problem by vehemently admonishing such an approach to female children and women in general.

The Prophet of Islam created a new culture that respected women in practice. For example, as a sign of respect for his daughter, Fatima, he rose up whenever she came into his presence and spread his robe on the floor for her to sit on. This behavior was completely at odds with the prevalent culture at the time. Although people objected to his respectful treatment of women, the Prophet was adamant in his attempts to create this novel culture.

The following saying from the Prophet clearly reflects the essence of the Islamic viewpoint and its respect for women: "No one respects women but the noblest amongst us and no one humiliates them but the depraved."

Prophet Muhammad paved the way for women and especially the most oppressed among them, the female slaves, to take part in social struggles almost 14 centuries ago. Soon, he managed to bring together a large population made up of hundreds of female pioneers whose names have been documented. The first person to die from torture in defense of Muhammad was a female slave named Somayya.

From the early days, women partook in duties regarded as very un-usual for them in that era: participation in political and social affairs. According to notable Islamic sources, over 600 vanguard women directly aligned themselves with the Prophet. Liberated from the control of their husbands and other men, they pledged their loyalty directly to the Prophet. This agreement was called *bay'at* and these women are referred to as *mobaye'at* in historical texts.[1]

Almost ten years after the advent of Islam, numerous new rules were gradually devised for all women, the study of which reveals a re-markable trend.

The history of early Islam also attests to the fact that a considerable number of commanders of Imam Ali's units and divisions in the War of Saffain were women. In the generation that followed, Zeinab Kobra, the sister of Imam Hussein and the daughter of Fatima and Ali, led the movement at its most critical juncture.[2]

---

1. *Mobaye'at* were vanguard women who emerged from among the first generations of Muslims, whose numbers were few. The names of more than 600 female personalities have been recorded in history and are called the "pledging women." The most famous and oldest sources of Islamic history have conducted independent studies of this issue and compiled a list of *Mobaye'at* women. The 7th volume of *Al-Tabaghat al-Kobra* by Ibn Saad is entirely devoted to the biographies of these women.

Similar numbers are mentioned in other credible sources such as *Al-Asabat fi Mo'arefat ol-Sahabeh,* written by Ibn Hajar and others.

These women not only abided by daily prayers, fasting and other rituals observed by Muslim women, but also undertook particular responsibilities before the Prophet, which were known as *bay'at* (pledge of allegiance). According to the Quran (Surat 60, verse 12), these vanguard women–without any form of family or tribal relation or dependency on men–had independently pledged not to leave the Prophet alone in any activity on the movement's agenda.

By relying on the teachings of the Prophet, these women, who had risen from various social strata including the slaves and the rich dynasties of Quraish, managed to undertake the most difficult responsibilities in the camps, battlefields and most importantly, in political and social arenas.

2. Ali ibn Abi Talib (Imam Ali) was the cousin and son-in-law of Islamic prophet Muhammad. He was also the first male convert to Islam. Fatima was the daughter of Prophet Muhammad and the wife of Ali. Zeinab and Hussein were among their children. Imam Hussein became the third Shiite Imam.

Several fundamental issues are in order in this respect:

WOMEN'S EQUAL RIGHT TO LIFE AND DIGNITY

Before the advent of Islam, women were oftentimes murdered on the slightest suspicion by the men in their family or tribe. The Quran explicitly banned this crime in The Isra'.

But was it only in Arabia that these crimes took place and a woman's right to life trampled upon? No. This was a universal occurrence in that era. Historical evidence documenting the most important civilizations of that era–Iran, Rome, China and India–indicates that aside from female slaves who, in a formal sense, had absolutely no rights to their life and destiny, other women were also virtually made into sexual slaves for men. During the time in Iran, Sassanid kings kept thousands of women detained in their harems. Meanwhile, women in other cities and villages were subjected to attacks and rape by greater and lesser rulers.[3]

WOMEN'S EQUAL HUMAN VALUE

To acknowledge women's human worth in particular, it is first necessary to assess the value of human beings in general according to

---

3. It is said that the haram of the Sasanid King, Khosrow I, with its 12,000 women and men, was considered one of the largest. Some times, rulers faced difficulties in handling the affairs of so many women. Hundreds and perhaps thousands of women were "detained" for one man and deprived of the opportunity to marry. The same was true of women and girls who were in the smaller harems of the rich and elite. All of these women were deprived of their social lives and were not actually counted as being among the living. In some societies, this caused shortages of women and led to added poverty. It was at this age, when (Iranian revolutionary) Mazdak demanded "distribution of women" and equal conditions for the rich and poor. He and thousands of his followers, however, were killed and defeated and the deplorable conditions of women continued. Under the Sasanid Dynasty, princes, Zoroastrian priests and even village headmen and landlords raided the residences of beautiful women and took them out of their husbands' houses. Will Durant narrated shameful stories in this regard in *The Story of Civilization.*

Islam. The Quran says all things have been created for humans and placed under their control.

According to The Cow, "It is He Who hath created for you all things that are on earth…"

The Isra' most explicitly states: "We have honored the sons of Adam; provided them with transport on land and sea; given them for sustenance things good and pure; and conferred on them special favors, above a great part of our creation."

From Islam's perspective, all human beings are equal regardless of their gender, race or ethnicity. The most fundamental values are those that relate to human attributes and righteous deeds. In Chapter Hojorat (The Apartments), the Quran does not attribute any value to sexual, racial or tribal differences, but instead points out that the highest value is "piety" (taqwa).[4]

The criterion for piety, or taqwa, concerns the special attributes of human beings that result from their ability to gain knowledge as well as their freedom of choice, both of which require them to be responsible.

Gender equality is one of the most obvious aspects of monotheistic anthropology. Over 90 percent of the verses in the Quran deal with ontology, history, and human responsibility, and do not differentiate at all between men and women.

The Quran addresses its audience as "O' you who believe" or "O' People," using the words Nass (people) and Bani Adam (humankind). This is also another indication that there is no gender discrimination in this holy book and that differentiation is completely

---

4. This essential principle is stated in verse 13 of The Inner Apartments: "O mankind! We created you from a single (pair) of a male and a female, and made you into nations and tribes, that ye may know each other. Verily the most honoured of you in the sight of Allah is (he who is) the most pious of you. And Allah has full knowledge and is well acquainted (with all things)."

a side issue. Of course, the much more important issue is the verses' content. Many of the verses of the Quran are explicit and unambiguous in indicating the equality of men and women in creation, and by implication, their equal worth and responsibilities. Throughout the Quran, the equality of women and men and their joint responsibilities are uniquely and strongly emphasized. In hundreds of instances, the Quran addresses both genders in the same way and without differentiating.

Although there are physiological differences between men and women, fundamentalists use these differences as the basis for human attributes. In this view, woman is a weak and unstable being who is constantly humiliated in comparison to man. Her indisputable rights as a human being are not recognized in the social, political and economic spheres and she is eventually condemned to a life of social isolation by being confined to her home.

In all realms of the fundamentalist value system, discrimination, war, suppression and bloodshed are all deemed superior values. Women are considered wicked and evil and men inherently corruptible. For this reason, the only way to achieve the reactionaries' desirable "purity" is through bloodshed, killing and death. In the final analysis, they see wickedness as the intrinsic characteristic of humans while spite, hostility, deceit, dishonesty and other negative qualities are regarded as their dominant drives.

Indeed, in a worldview where women are considered second-class citizens deprived of their genuine rights, how could the men themselves claim to be free and avoid doubting their own humanity? Everyone proves his or her humanity in a social context and over the course of relations with others. So, are men not in some sense also captives and slaves themselves? The answer is yes. Yes, because they themselves have been shackled by instituting their tyrannical hegemony over women and inevitably, over society and history.

The monotheist ideology, however, neither values men's physical power or desire for supremacy nor women's physical weakness and femininity. This ideology uses more solid criteria such as consciousness, freedom of choice and responsibility, all of which are considered essential human attributes, to view both men and women. This is where a woman finds her strong, independent and completely equal personality and is identified as such. In the monotheist ideology, men and women are both equally in need of one another and neither one is considered as secondary to the other.

This ideology has its own value system and its highest values are life, love, compassion, generosity, sacrifice, trust and honesty. The deficiencies and actual physical differences in gender or race are not of much importance. Although these differences are real, they are of minor significance and should not prevent anyone's progress. In light of this monotheist outlook, almost 14 centuries ago, the Prophet of Islam addressed women on equal footing with men in his invitation to believe in God. It is no coincidence that the first believer and the first martyr of Islam were both women. Of the nine first believers who joined the Prophet, three were women.

The Quran says humankind is God's heir on Earth. The Quran puts great women like the Virgin Mary on par with the prophets because they were given great historical responsibilities. The Quran has chosen for its role models for humanity from among women such as Assiya[5] and Hajar[6], a development that leads to Khadija and Fatima[7] in the age of Islam.

---

5. Assiya (also known as Asiya bint Muzahim) was among the leading women mentioned in the Quran. She was the wife of the Pharaoh who reigned during Moses's time. The Quran reveres her as a strong woman who refused to lose faith in God even though she was married to one of the most evil men in history.

6. Hajar (or Hagar) was an Egyptian handmaid, who married Abraham and gave birth to Ishmael (Isaac).

7. Khadija was Prophet Muhammad's wife. Fatima was the Prophet's daughter. Khadija was the first convert to Islam.

GENDER EQUALITY BASED ON THE REJECTION OF EXPLOITATION

The fundamentalists justify various forms of discrimination and inequality, including gender discrimination, in the name of Islam. Underlying their justifications is the acceptance of exploitation.

Democratic Islam, however, believes in monotheism and the rejection of exploitation. It seeks to realize the ideal of equality and emancipation from all forms of discrimination and bondage. Islam's social ideal is the realization of freedom, justice and social unity. In The Iron, the Quran says the philosophy behind the introduction of the prophets is to create justice and what it refers to as "*Qest,*" which marks the highest phase of freedom, justice and social unity.[8]

In such a society, the oppressed and those with suppressed talents will be free and able to take positions that allow them to utilize their fullest potentials.

The Prophets in the Quran promise emancipation from oppression and discrimination, saying, "My servants, the righteous, shall inherit the earth."

EQUALITY IN SOCIAL AFFAIRS

In the beginning of the Prophet's mission, all women were invited to Islam one by one, independent of their male "masters" and regardless of who their husbands, fathers or mothers were. Women were allowed to decide for themselves whether to accept or reject the invitation.

Women's pioneering role in the political struggle, which came about without having to first receive the permission of their husbands or other male members of their families, was recognized. We know that

---

8. The Iron, verse 25: "We sent aforetime our apostles with Clear Signs and sent down with them the Book and the Balance (of Right and Wrong), that men may stand forth in justice."

even today in the Third World, many girls are not allowed to engage in political activity without their families' permission. The Prophet, however, accepted women's decisions to follow Islam, which was considered a political movement at the time. They could make this choice equally as well as men could, thereby putting an end to all forms of inequality. This freedom was extended to all women, from the noble Hashemite and Quraish tribes to female slaves.

The Prophet also supported women's *hijra* (migration), despite opposition from their fathers. Furthermore, a number of women who had converted to Islam were called upon to migrate from their countries, while others were encouraged to engage in *jihad* (holy war) and were given comparable shares from the war booty as men.

Under Prophet Mohammad and even after his death, a woman's right to testify in financial deals and before the courts was recognized. Later on, a woman's testimony was widely trusted and even became a common practice in religious affairs as well.

SUPPORTING WOMEN IN FAMILY RELATIONS

Prior to the dawn of Islam, women and girls did not have any rights as they pertained to whom they could choose to marry. Under Islam, women were granted the right to negotiate and come to an agreement about any conditions that they deemed necessary for their future. A woman's equal right in setting conditions in marriage has been emphasized in the Quran in The Women (*Nisa*). Contrary to the methods of other religions or during the era of ignorance, marriage became a purely social contract, devoid of any religious or metaphysical aura. In marriage, both sides have the right to set any condition they see appropriate and come to a mutual understanding. These conditions may include custody over children, employment, place of residence, divorce or any other issues related to married life. There is a general consensus that a marriage is considered void without the woman's consent.

In this way, a woman's right to voluntarily marry was recognized while any form of compulsion or reluctance by her father or elders was forbidden. Consider that even now, in many societies, including in Iran, girls are not permitted to marry without the permission and blessing of their families. Islam also prohibited risky pregnancies, any form of compulsory service at home and even forcibly breast-feeding newborns.

An important step in favor of women was the abolition of oppressive and arbitrary types of divorce that were common practice at the time. Many men divorced their wives without the slightest justification. In one of the more oppressive forms of divorce called "*Zihar,*" husbands effectively played games with the fate of their wives when betting, gambling or entering into financial deals. One man might promise, for example, to pay his debt on time, to make his camel deliver on time or kill someone, adding that if he could not perform these actions, then "my wife would replace my mother." As such, the fate of a woman was oftentimes determined by something as arbitrary as a man's ability to win or lose a bet!

Another form of oppressive divorce was called "*Ila'a,*" in which the husband vowed to boycott his wife without officially divorcing her. Effectively, the woman was turned into a prisoner who had to remain inside of her husband's house. Another oppressive tradition was called "*ta'aliq*" whereby the man left his wife without divorcing her. As a result, the woman could not go on with her life and re-marry, for example. Islam denounced and annulled these oppressive and extremely misogynistic forms of divorce (See Chapter Mojadela, verse 58).

Another major step in the restitution of women's rights came when Islam granted them the right to request a divorce according to their own volition. The first divorce requested by a woman without seeking her husband's consent was carried out by the Prophet himself, and was subsequently endorsed and documented in the Quran (second verse of Chapter Baghara [Cow]). This type of divorce is called "*khol'e.*" In this particular instance, a woman called Habibeh, daughter of Sohal, was married to a man by the name of Sabet, son of Ghays. Habibeh complained to the Prophet that she no longer wanted to live with her husband because she did not like him. The Prophet asked her several questions and then carried out the divorce without requiring her to engage in any discussions with her husband.

FINANCIAL AND ECONOMIC AFFAIRS

As stated in The Women, the Quran emphasizes a woman's right to equal and unconditional ownership. Prior to Islam, women were essentially perceived as the assets of their husbands or male family members. Even their jewelry and belongings were considered possessions that could be taken away from them if the man wished to do so. Islam recognized a woman's full right to ownership without any difference from men. Women also enjoyed full and equal rights to sign any social or economic contract.

Aside from a few exceptions and the lifestyle prevalent among the aristocrats, Arab tribes did not recognize a woman's right to own or inherit property.

When the law governing women's inheritance was transmitted in the form of verses in the Quran, many of the Prophet's followers protested. They argued that wealth would be wasted in the hands of women.

WOMEN'S COMPETENCE IN LEADERSHIP

In my view, women's status in political and social leadership roles is the most important issue in the confrontation between the fundamentalists and Islam. In the fundamentalist outlook, women are always and eternally deprived of the right to leadership and participation in government and also political power-sharing. They do not have the right to be judges or sources of religious guidance and instruction. In the logic of the fundamentalist mullahs, it is very obvious that the issue is not about knowledge or competence but is rather based on the mere fact that the person is a woman.

Mullah Mohammad Yazdi, a former head of the Iranian regime's Judiciary and one of Khamenei's close confidants, clearly declares, "In (Khomeini's) Islam, women are prohibited from two things. One is judgment and the other is authority (i.e. right to rule). Regardless of the extent of knowledge, virtue, superiority and discretion, a woman cannot rule because of the fact that she is a woman."

In democratic Islam, however, women and men are equally qualified and dedicated in undertaking leadership roles in society, an ideal that is extracted from the letter of the Quran and Islam. In The Repentance, the Quran explicitly notes, "The believers, men and women, are no different and are both guardians and protectors of one another..."[9]

The term "protector" used in this verse gives rise to a very important concept because it carries with it the meaning of guardianship and leadership. This is synonymous with having limitless love for fellow human beings and accepting responsibility for them.

---

9. Repentance, verse 71: "The Believers, men and women, are protectors one of another: they enjoin what is just, and forbid what is evil: they observe regular prayers, practise regular charity, and obey Allah and His Messenger. On them will Allah pour His mercy: for Allah is Exalted in power, Wise."

This concept has been expressed in the Quran in other forms as well. In The Family of Imran, it is said that women and men are created from the same body and the worth of their efforts is equal.

According to the Quran, the equality of women and men in carrying out their responsibilities and in morality is comprehensive. In The Clans we read, "For Muslim men and women, for believing men and women, for devout men and women, for true men and women, for men and women who are patient, for compassionate and humble men and women, for men and women who give to charity, for men and women who fast (and deny themselves), for men and women who guard their chastity, and for men and women who engage much in Allah's praise, for them Allah has prepared forgiveness and great reward."

Despite such indisputable evidence, Iran's ruling fundamentalists have officially prohibited women from undertaking their most important social responsibilities, including participation in the judiciary, religious stewardship, leadership and governmental affairs.

According to Article 115 of the clerical regime's constitution, the president must be chosen from among religious men.

As a Muslim woman, I declare that these claims run contrary to Islam. Under Islam, women enjoy all these rights and share the same privileges as men. The mullahs' unfounded arguments for denying women the right to judge, as well as the ability to hold religious and social leadership positions, stem from common references. By talking primarily about judicial roles they subsequently came to the conclusion to ban women from holding governance, social and religious leadership positions.

So, if their reasons for depriving women of judicial positions are not credible, then the claims on prohibiting women from religious leadership, governance and social leadership are automatically rendered specious and baseless.

In religious jurisprudence, every precept and theory is evaluated by employing the following four criteria:

1. The Quran;

2. The Tradition of the Prophet and Imams, including their sayings, writings and conduct;

3. The consensus opinion among scholars;

4. Common sense.

The reasoning that the mullahs use in the attempt to prove their claims, however, is not compatible with any of the above criteria:

1. **In the context of the Quran:** There is no verse in the Quran that bans women from assuming the position of a judge, from being a religious or social leader, or from participating in governance. On the contrary, when the Quran speaks of judgment and leadership, it addresses both men and women generally: "God doth command you to render back your trusts to those to whom they are due; and when yea judge between people, that yea judge with justice." (The Women, verse 58)

   In other verses, including verse 71 of The Repentance and verse 74 of The Criterion, the Quran underscores women's social responsibility and their right to lead precisely in conjunction with men.

2. **In the context of the Tradition:** None of the mullahs' references show that the Prophet barred women from being judges or participating in governance. Conversely, we know that during the time of the Rashidin caliphs and afterwards, everyone considered women's "narrations" from the Prophet as credible

while many of them became incorporated into the books of narrations (*hadith*).

The mullahs' verbal citations that seek to prove that Islam bans women from judgment or leadership positions are unfounded. For example, they argue that if a woman were to become a judge, men would be driven to sin after hearing her voice whenever she spoke. This is the type of logic that the mullahs use to argue against permitting women from sitting on the bench.

Such reasoning is both absurd and implausible. Did women like Umma Salma not provide their own narratives of the Tradition of the Prophet? Did the Prophet's daughter and granddaughter, Fatima and Zeinab, respectively, not deliver elaborate sermons in public and in mosques?

3. **In the context of consensus opinion:** Contrary to the belief that all religious scholars are in agreement about barring women from holding leadership and judgment positions, many of the most prominent Sunni scholars, including Abu Hanifeh,[10] see no reason for these restrictions. Mohammad Jarir Tabari, a prominent jurist and author of the acclaimed *Tabari History*,[11] also says, "Since women are allowed to master *Ijtihad*, they can also become judges in all affairs, just like men."

The consensus among Shiite scholars over prohibiting women from judgment is also very doubtful. Shiekh Mohammad Hassan An-Najafi, author of *Jawaher-ol Kalam (The Gems of Discourse)*, cites "consensus" as proof that judges must be male. However, one of the most prominent Shiite jurists, Allameh Hilli,[12] wrote in his book *Nahj-ol Haq (The Road to Truth)* that

---

10. Abu Hanifeh, leader of the largest branch of Sunni Muslims, died in 793 A.D.

11. Tabari died in 953 A.D.

12. Hilli died in 1405 A.D.

there is no consensus about the "male" precondition. Hossein Ali Montazeri, Khomeini's onetime designated successor and whose special credibility as a jurist Khomeini repeatedly emphasized, rejected Najafi's contention that there is even a consensus in this regard. In his book, The *Religious Foundations of Islamic Government*, Montazeri writes: "In all the books I have studied which use citations from the infallible Imams, I have not encountered such a contention." The existence of serious disagreement among religious scholars makes it clear that there is no specific citation in the Prophet's Tradition or *Hadith* which would bar women from assuming judgment and thereby leadership roles.

4. **In the context of common sense:** A simple question can be enlightening for any Muslim: How could it be possible that women and men bear equal religious and social responsibility to propagate the faith and are equally obliged by the Quran to promote justice and monotheism (*Towhid*), while at the same time, when it comes to the most crucial means of advancing these objectives, i.e. religious leadership, women are excluded? Why should women who master *Ijtihad* be deprived of the right to religious leadership in the same way as lunatics and criminals, even though they may be superior to others in this regard, and why should others be deprived of the opportunity for greater insight and understanding of the religion? We are free to debate at length about the qualifications required by any woman or man for occupying the position of religious leadership, judgeship and social leadership. But, on what logical basis can one deny women the opportunity to acquire religious qualifications and knowledge?

According to the criteria of jurisprudence, being a man is not a precondition for becoming a judge or a leader. Contrary to what the fundamentalists attribute to Islam and based on the logic of the

Quran, women can both become a judge or religious leader and also undertake leadership positions.

In fact, the main contradiction in the claims made by religious fundamentalists and what subsequently invalidates them, is that they turn God's religion and book, which according to all Muslims and in the words of the Prophet, is the guide for all Muslim generations, into a static and soulless set of rules. In the words of Imam Ali, their interpretation of Islam and the Quran has nothing in common with Islam or the Quran. In *Nahj-ol Balagha (The Road to Eloquence)*, Imam Ali predicts a time that is astonishingly similar to the present circumstances under the mullahs' regime in Iran. He says, "There will come a day when the mosques have flourishing exteriors and facades, but have been corrupted in their power for guidance. There will come a day when those who build the mosques and those who attend them are the worst kinds of people on Earth."[13]

FIGHTING A MALE-DOMINATED CULTURE

Islam has not remained content with merely paving the way for women; it has also formulated explicit rules to block the aggressive nature of male domination. It has tried to institute significant prohibitions intended to block the aggressive habits and unbridled exploitation that the ruling classes propagate on the basis of their interests.

For example, as stated in The Isra', the Quran made sexual exploitation unlawful. This decree was made amidst the already gloomy destiny of all women who were threatened by sexual exploitation in one of the most impoverished parts of the world.

Another order in this regard was declaring it a crime to harass women. The Quran deals with the issue of husbands' harassment of their

---

13. *Nahj-ol Balagha* (The Road to Eloquence), sermon 361

wives. After recommending and stressing peaceful methods, the Quran clearly forbids men from leaving their wives with uncertain futures and recommends separation instead. (Recall that before the emergence of Islam in Arabia, men legally owned the bodies of their wives).

The slandering of women is also regarded as a crime, as pointed out in The Light. Unfounded slandering of women is among the few cardinal sins, on a par with murder and polytheism, and is a punishable offense, even if the offender is the woman's husband.[14]

Furthermore, Islam restricted and prohibited polygamy. Before the advent of Islam, it was considered an honor for renowned men to have an unrestricted number of wives. It signified wealth, power and a means to have more children, potential soldiers who could fight for the head of the tribe in tribal wars.

From the outset, Islam placed restrictions on polygamy, reducing the number of wives a man could have to four and, despite outrage among renowned men, it forced them to divorce their additional wives. On the other hand, it set conditions that made the practice of having more than one wife difficult. The most important of these conditions was to maintain justice among any number of wives. The Quran reiterated in The Women, "Ye shall never be able to deal justly (with them)."[15]

---

14. As mentioned in various verses in Light, the Quran believes that women who are subjects of oppressive accusations must be defended in special ways. In the case of women who are accused by their husbands–contrary to the past when the husband was free to murder his wife under the pretext of "defending his dignity"—the accusing husband is deprived of his wife. The protocol for this separation is a ceremony where the man and woman make mutual vows denying or confirming the charge. It is understandable that this law was drawn entirely in favor of women.

15. The Women, verse 3: "If ye fear that ye shall not be able to deal justly with the orphans, Marry women of your choice, Two or three or four; but if ye fear that ye shall not be able to deal justly (with them), then only one, or (a captive) that your right hands possess, that will be more suitable, to prevent you from doing injustice."

The fundamentalists defend polygamy today by citing Islamic precepts dating back 1,400 years. This is another example of the reactionary dogmatism that, needless to say, adheres to the wicked ambitions of the male-dominated regime.

In view of the Quran's dynamism and the spirit and direction of the order that restricted the number of wives one could have, we believe polygamy is a perversion that runs counter to Islam's emancipating spirit.

By bringing up these examples, I have aimed to demonstrate that what Islam has historically granted women, namely human status as well as social, economic and political rights, were extraordinarily revolutionary in and of themselves. Giving a share of inheritance to women, recognizing their right to own private property (at a time when they were absolutely excluded from the economic cycle) and recognizing their right to testimony, judgeship and leadership, were each considered major leaps forward at the time and remained unprecedented even in the centuries that followed.

THE ROADMAP

Another question that arises in this discussion is whether the privileges that women gained in those times meant complete equality. Obviously, not! However, although those privileges did not result in complete equality for women, each one constituted a major qualitative step forward 14 centuries ago. Without a belief in equality, granting such rights to women would have been irrelevant. The said rights were in fact part of a phased movement towards complete equality. When we look at the dynamic logic of the Quran, we discover that these privileges establish a roadmap for emancipation and equality.

This reality becomes all the more obvious when we note that women in the most advanced contemporary societies, even several centuries following the advent of Islam, still did not enjoy the rights that Islam prescribed for women.

For consecutive centuries in Britain, women were considered legally on par with the insane. A law adopted in 1882 excluded women from that category. In Germany, a civil code adopted in 1900 declared that women should enjoy the same rights as their husbands. In France, a law enacted on February 18, 1938 annulled a previous one that regarded married women as being of inferior status.

Women gradually gained equal economic and social rights in European countries only during the following decades. Nonetheless, European communities have yet to take any significant steps regarding women's participation in political leadership.

So, even if one were to compare today's achievements with those of women in the early days of Islam, one would acknowledge that Islam brought about a major leap forward in the lives of women.

So the question is: Are we supposed to use as our model the tactical rules that appeared to be progressive 1,400 years ago? Naturally, the answer is no! Those were merely tactical achievements meant for making progress from an old era to a new one. Today, it would be reactionary and unacceptable to keep the old forms. Adherence to the genuine spirit of Islam necessitates that women enjoy equal rights and freedoms within the social and economic developments of the current era. So, what counts is the humane message of Mohammed's faith and equality for all humankind, be it men or women.

Based on this belief, and inspired by Mohammadan Islam, women of the Iranian resistance have found their pioneering role in the movement, stepping into the frontlines of the battle against Islamic fundamentalism.

5

Status of Iranian Women

WOMEN IN THE 2009 REVOLTS

In June 2009, an uprising erupted in Iran when factional disputes during the course of the sham presidential elections led to a rift at the top of the *Velayat-e Faqih* regime (absolute rule of the clergy). The uprising expanded from Tehran to at least 30 other cities across the country and turned into the most significant sociopolitical development since the beginning of the mullahs' rule in Iran.

From the outset, analysts were so impressed by the role Iranian women played in the uprising that some called it a "women's revolution."

Iranian women participated on a large scale in anti-government protests and played an active role in the social networks that organized the demonstrations. They bravely stood up to the Islamic Revolutionary Guards' raids, encouraged others to take part in the protests and attended to the wounded. Mothers regularly gathered in different locations around Tehran to inspire people to carry on with the uprising for freedom.

Numerous young women were imprisoned during this period and resisted even when faced with torture and various forms of humiliating treatment. Others organized and led groups of protesters. It is no accident that Neda Agha-Sultan became the symbol of the Iranian people's uprising and scenes of her death inspired respect for and solidarity with the people of Iran across the world. Women's involvement in the uprising was a sign of its progressive nature and its demand to topple the mullahs was, to a great extent, a reflection of women's impact on the movement.

An objective study of the events will lead one to recognize that women played a decisive role in the protests. This proves once again that women are the answer to the challenges presented by religious fascism and Islamic fundamentalism and that the defeat of fundamentalism will be made possible by women.

Anyone remotely familiar with Iran's ruling dictatorship may be surprised to see this position of Iranian women, considering the fact that the country is ruled by a medieval regime whose most prominent attribute is misogyny. This is a regime that carries out the cruelest forms of torture as well as some of the most inhumane punishments, such as stoning and the gouging out of eyes. Specifically, these types of suppressive measures target women.

As such, Iranian women's prominent role in the struggle for freedom is a question mark for many. Clearly, this role did not come about overnight. In fact, three fundamental elements have led to Iranian women's current position at the frontlines: their experience in the political struggle, the misogyny of the ruling regime and the presence of an organized resistance with women's equality as its ideal.

Tehran: protests of 2009

FIRST FACTOR: STRUGGLE FOR FREEDOM AND EQUALITY

Iranian women have a 150-year history of struggling for equality and opposing dictatorship. This experience has put Iranian women in a progressive position both culturally and intellectually.

Iranian women have played significant roles in three major movements in the 20th century: the Constitutional Revolution (1906), the Oil Nationalization Movement (1950s) and the anti-monarchic revolution (1979).

In 1875, when the Qajar King Nassereddin Shah gave exclusive rights to tobacco production and sales to the British firm Regie, the people vehemently protested and boycotted the use of tobacco, forcing the king to annul the agreement. Iranian women were at the forefront of this popular movement. Even within the Royal Court, women rose up against the agreement, breaking hookahs and joining the boycott.

In the 1906 Constitutional Revolution, which resulted in the adoption of a constitution and the creation of a parliament, Iranian women had a remarkable presence and even participated in the armed struggle at the time. Because of the Constitutional Revolution and its consequent achievements, women were admitted into schools, schools for girls were established and women's societies sprang up, in addition to the publication of the first Iranian magazine for women.[1]

---

1. William Morgan Shuster, an American who lived in Iran in the early 20th century, wrote in 1912 in his book, *The Strangling of Persia*: "The Persian women since 1907 had become almost at a bound the most progressive, not to say radical, in the world. That this statement upsets the ideas of centuries makes no difference. It is the fact. It is not too much to say that without the powerful moral force of those women… the ill-starred and short-lived revolutionary movement… would have early paled into a more disorganized protest. The women did much to keep the spirit of liberty alive. Having themselves suffered from a double form of oppression, political and social, they were the more eager to foment the great Nationalist movement… In their struggle for liberty and its modern expressions, they broke through some of the most sacred customs which for centuries past have bound their sex in the land of Iran." See William Morgan Shuster, *The Strangling of Persia*, Mage Publishers, 1987, pp. 191-192.
On December 1, 1911, the Association of Women of the Homeland staged a demonstration

Women's participation in the Constitutional Revolution began through their financial donations to the cause, arousing a sense of patriotism in gatherings and taking part in marches. Underground and semi-underground councils and societies gradually took shape in major cities and women began organizing activities to advance the revolution.

When the newly-established Majlis (Parliament) decided to set up the National Bank without borrowing from foreign governments, women enthusiastically raised a considerable amount of money and even donated their own jewelry. Women's role in the city of Tabriz was particularly noteworthy. When the Qajar King, Mohammad-Ali Shah, shelled the parliament and constitutionalists were being gunned down, women handled all the affairs behind the lines in the 11-month siege against the city. Among other things, for example, they raised money, carried food from fort to fort, treated the wounded and prepared the ammunitions.

A group of women also fought on the frontlines. Among them were women and girls who wore men's clothing while fighting alongside them.

Women's sit-in in 1906 Constitutional movement

by thousands of women in front of the Majlis (parliament). Shuster wrote that a group of some 300 women entered the parliament… "These cloistered Persian mothers, wives and daughters exhibited threateningly their revolvers, tore aside their veils, and confessed their decision to kill their own husbands and sons, and leave them behind their own dead bodies, if the deputies wavered in their duty to uphold the liberty and dignity of the Persian people and nation."(*Ibid*, p. 198).

Half a century later in the midst of the struggle in the late 1940s and beginning of 1950s, especially during the Oil Nationalization Movement led by Dr. Mohammad Mossadeq, Iranian women lent their unremitting and significant support to the movement.

Women's demonstration in Tehran with the motto of "We must intervene in the country's politics" – Tehran, 1943

Women participation in the 1979 anti-monarchy revolution

In the struggle against the dictatorship just prior to 1979, women, alongside men, actively demanded freedom and democracy. Female students, in particular, were actively involved in social and political groups and associations. On the whole, women were active on a very large scale during the 1979 revolution.

When the clerical regime seized power, it faced a society that wanted its historical demands met after 100 years of struggling for democracy. So, Iranian women relied on a long tradition in the movement for equality.

After the 1979 revolution, Iran had to pave the way towards a broad-based and democratic development, with women playing a prominent role. Khomeini, however, set up a fundamentalist and misogynous regime that attacked even the laws and reforms women had gradually gained over time.

Women's extensive presence in the 1979 anti-monarchic revolution

Immediately after the mullahs took power, they imposed compulsory *hijab* (veiling) and began expelling women from the workplace. Sexual discrimination and oppression was carried out without mercy. Iranian women rose up to resist and led the regime's opponents. They actively participated in opposition meetings, marches and demonstrations. Their active social presence, which included expressing their views on the most serious political issues of the day, especially the presence of Muslim women in the social arena, served as an arrow that struck at the heart of the ruling culture and reactionary ideology.

In a speech delivered at the European Parliament on February 23, 2010, Mrs. Maryam Rajavi presented a book containing pictures of 2,700 PMOI women executed by the clerical regime. This is part of the compiled list of names and particulars of 20,000 fallen members of the People's Mojahedin Organization of Iran (a pivotal force in the Iranian opposition movement). The total number of those executed in Iran on political grounds under the mullahs' regime exceeds 120,000.

In this way, Iranian women's life and death struggle against the ruling fundamentalists began in 1981 and has continued ever since. What we say today about Islamic fundamentalism and women as the answer and the antithesis to fundamentalism relies on three decades of experience on this path.

It was very difficult for a regime that rules in the name of Islam to see the Muslim PMOI and especially the organization's female supporters stand at the forefront of its opponents. To fight such a monster, women had to overcome extremely difficult obstacles in a traditional society ruled by a religious dictatorship. Most of the time, the first obstacle was a woman's family and parents. Women had to forgo their education, husbands and children to join the struggle. In the fight against a ruthless regime that even hangs children, there was no place for family life, especially for those who were on the frontlines.

In addition, in contrast to men, women had to endure the cynicism, insults and humiliation for taking part in the struggle. So, they needed to muster up the ability to overcome such hardships. For example people used to say:

- These women have abandoned their parents, sisters and brothers because they have no affection;

- Can women participate in the struggle and be effective against such a regime?

- It is better for women to take care of their family and children; who else would do these chores in their absence?

- Once women are arrested and sent to prisons and torture chambers, their families will be humiliated.

200,000-strong rally called by the PMOI against the killing of two female sympathizers by Khomeini's revolutionary guards - Tehran, April 27, 1981

Despite such ranting, however, the extensive participation of women in the struggle against religious fascism created a new culture in Iranian society. Many parents joined the struggle, along with their sons and daughters, against religious fascism and sacrificed their lives in the process. Women's broad participation in the resistance against religious fundamentalism is in itself a sign of this struggle's inevitable victory.

Women's protests against the post-revolutionary government

The sign reads: "Freedom of women is freedom of society" Meanwhile, the mullahs' propaganda machine began a campaign of demagoguery and charlatanism that would surpass even the likes of Hitler's propaganda chief Josef Goebbels. The regime orchestrated a campaign to discredit the politically active or PMOI women in order to stop others from joining the resistance. However, these efforts failed in the face of women's burning desire for equality and freedom. Women of the PMOI stood firm and proudly passed these grueling tests.

Tens of thousands of women were tortured and executed during this period in the confrontation with the religious dictatorship. In the process, stories of a great number of heroines and martyrs emerged, unprecedented in the history of the Iranian movement for democracy, especially in the torture chambers of the Khomeini regime. Among the executed were 13-year-old girls like Fatemeh Mesbah and elderly mothers like Mother Zakeri, along with a remarkable number of pregnant women who were ruthlessly sent before the firing squads. Many lost their lives through torture. The clerical regime has invented 174 forms of torture to break our prisoners.

These atrocities are of course very shocking but they speak to the strength and heroism the mullahs faced when dealing with these pioneering women. One can also understand how threatened the mullahs felt by their struggle. These women showed that they are the necessary answer to Islamic fundamentalism and religious tyranny and that without their presence in political leadership, it would be inconceivable to remain steadfast or realize the prospect for victory.

The mullahs have remained in power by resorting to the most violent forms of repression. But the reality is that the resistance's pioneering women have defeated their misogynous ideology and cleared the image of Islam from the stigma of inequality. They have proved in practice, the true face of Islam: its humanitarian nature, its conviction in women's equality and its message of tolerance, forgiveness, compassion and emancipation.

SECOND FACTOR: MULLAHS' MISOGYNY

The second element is the misogyny of the ruling regime that was already explained in the previous chapter. In fact, when the mullahs seized power in 1979, they could not tolerate women's activities because of their medieval ideology. Women's political and social activities laid the grounds for their higher demands for freedom, democracy and equality, which enjoyed profound and wide-ranging support in society and consequently defied the mullahs' rule. Hence the mullahs' constant need for suppression, which has turned Iran into a great prison for women. As such, the mullahs combine a political imperative (i.e. cracking down on the women's liberation movement and maintaining an atmosphere of suppression over the entire society) with an ideological resolve (i.e. degradation and suppression of women, which forms the basis and foundation for their project).

THIRD FACTOR: ORGANIZED RESISTANCE

Plenary session of the National Council of Resistance,
the Iranian resistance's Parliament-in-exile

The third factor is the existence of an organized resistance with deep roots in Iranian society. The movement's adherence to women's equality and its historical initiative in accepting women's leadership resulted in a leap forward in the advancement of the cause of equality in Iranian society. The pivotal force of this movement is the People's Mojahedin Organization of Iran (PMOI), whose conviction in a tolerant Islam and in the cause of equality has had a great impact on Muslim women and men not only in Iran but also in other countries of the region.

Currently, 52 percent of the more than 500 members of the Resistance's Parliament[2] are women. They comprise the majority of

2. The National Council of Resistance of Iran is a broad-based coalition of various political tendencies in Iran and represents a considerable part of Iranian society. It is considered the largest, most lasting coalition in the history of Iran. The NCRI was founded in 1981 by Massoud Rajavi. Representatives of various political groups and trends, religious and national minorities, various social strata including artists, athletes as well as intellectuals are members of the NCRI, which is the only alternative to the mullahs' regime and seeks to end tyranny in Iran. It also seeks to establish a republic based on secularism, pluralism, equality of the sexes and advocates annihiliation of death penalty and a non-nuclear Iran.

The National Council of Resistance of Iran has pioneered the struggle to reject the clerical regime in its entirety while the council's positions on the *Velayat-e faqih* regime's lack of capacity for reform and internal change have been proven right.

By exposing the clerical regime's secret nuclear sites in 2002 and at least another 80 instances of senior officials in Ashraf (the Iranian opposition's base in Iraq located 70 km from the Iranian border). For more than a decade, the PMOI's all-women leadership council has, with competence and hegemony, led the organization that bears the movement's most serious responsibilities. They have gained extensive experience as a result.

---

divulging the details of the mullahs' nuclear arms program, the NCRI has played a significant role in attracting international attention to the regime's nuclear threat.

6

The Iranian
Resistance's Experience

As far as women's particular history in confronting Islamic fundamentalism is concerned, there are a number of essential issues that
could, at the very least, be presented as a valuable experience to
women around the world. The basic lesson of the Iranian women's
experience in confronting these enemies of humanity can be summed
up by their refusal to compromise with this inhuman regime in its
entirety and in maintaining a decisive and solid boundary.

Women's presence in the resistance's leadership has been attained
throughout the course of the confrontation with a regime that will
never recognize any rights for women in leadership, government
and politics. The mullahs have been and continue to be determined
to eradicate the human dignity of Iranian women. One of the most
important factors in our success was that we correctly grasped this
reality. Of course, we paid a heavy price for it. Yet because of this
correct understanding, we made progress in the right direction. The
price was immense but the outcome was extraordinary. The price
was the lives of thousands upon thousands of pioneering women
from among the purest, bravest and most knowledgeable people in
Iran. The price was to endure the most cruel types of torture and
the agony of the struggle as well as the resistance endured by thousands of unknown women in its ranks who sacrificed everything

they had to achieve freedom. They remained steadfast even in the face of unimaginable conditions. But thanks to a profound cultural struggle within the movement against all the remnants of reactionary thought, women today have made great, and sometimes unique, achievements in the Iranian resistance when compared with all other liberation movements.

A KEY QUESTION THAT LED TO A MAJOR CHANGE

In 1985, our movement was faced with a crucial question while evaluating its annual reports. The question was, "Why had women's level of responsibility remained three tiers below men's in the People's Mojahedin Organization of Iran (as the pivotal force of the Resistance)?" This occurred while women were widely present in all aspects of the movement. Also, in light of the fact that the PMOI believed in women's equality as an ideological value and while there were practically no apparent obstacles or restrictions for women's advancement, why was it, then, that our women had stopped at this level?

This was an important question because we could not walk on one leg. We needed a transformation that could shatter the prevailing mentality and pave the way for a new way of thinking.

There were numerous debates about this issue. The topic had, of course, often preoccupied me throughout my political life. For years, ever since I became politically active, I had thought of how to open the way for women's emancipation. I think this question inevitably preoccupies every woman, although because of the complexity of the issue, it might sooner or later be abandoned. Nonetheless, this issue had become the subject of a collective debate at the level of a major resistance movement and I could feel the need for it from various aspects.

Different options lay before us as we tried to answer this question. Some suggested the increased participation of women in executive affairs so that they could gradually gain competence in different arenas and be able to undertake more senior responsibilities.

However, Massoud Rajavi, the leader of the Iranian resistance, believed that the solution should come from the top, through the participation of women in leadership so that the path would be opened for women's growth in all levels of the movement. This was a very inspirational solution, but immediately afterwards another question was raised: Was there a woman that could fulfill this responsibility?

When I was nominated to undertake this responsibility, I felt the weight of it on my shoulders and thought that the difficulties of making decisions about it were beyond my power. Making decisions was very difficult for me because from then on I had to accept the enormous responsibility of leading a movement that was struggling against a most appalling religious tyranny. Only one thought helped eliminate my doubts: I could see that in the objective world outside me and on the ground, it was necessary to take this step in order to advance the resistance movement towards equality, which had become indispensible to bringing change to Iran.

The motivation to do what was necessary for the sake of the reality that lay beyond me created the flickering of a new idea. That is, if I began from myself, it would be difficult and most probably not practical to find an answer. But, if I started from the responsibility before me—namely, the realization of freedom, democracy and equality in Iran—I had to accept the challenge in spite of all the adversities.

Later, in the course of the practical experience of confronting the ideology that thrives on gender discrimination and male domination, it was proven to us that emancipation from it would not be possible without novel humane motivations and insights. In addition, during several months of debate, I had felt that women's emancipation and the release of their energies, as well as my own emancipation, depended on accepting this responsibility. What happened in practice, however, was something none of us could have predicted.

REVOLT AGAINST GENDER DISCRIMINATION

The Mojahedin made the important discovery that if they wanted to stand up to religious tyranny, they would have to struggle against a patriarchal and reactionary system, namely, a gender-based ideology.

This ideological transformation emanated from the PMOI's anthropological views, which were diametrically opposed to Khomeini's reactionary views.

According to the PMOI worldview, human beings are born as men or as women. Thus, while they are not the same from a purely physiological perspective, they are equal in so far as they are both human beings.

In contrast, a gender-based ideology is based on the superiority and supremacy of males over females. This outlook finds its roots in the history and culture of oppression and objectification, that enslave women, men and all of society.

Therefore, a gender-based ideology is not intrinsic to the human species as such, and does not emanate from their instincts or their fundamental essence. It is rather constructed from behaviors, attitudes and a culture that is itself the product of oppression and exploitation.

In Khomeini's reactionary ideology, men discover their true identity through acts of suppression and in particular, their subjugation of women. They are driven and guided by this ideology.

In other words, in Khomeini's mindset, a man's character and identity is dependent upon his ability to suppress and exploit women. Without harboring a sense of superiority over women, he would feel unfulfilled and lacking true self-confidence.

In this ideology, women regard their subordination, reliance on men and second-class status as both rational and natural.

Consequently, the woman develops a quality alien to her genuine human nature; that is, the quality of a subject or a product whose worth is correlated only to its usefulness as a commodity for others.

To put it in another way, women are also enslaved by such attitudes towards themselves. As Simone de Beauvoir said, "One is not born, but rather becomes, a woman."

In reality, the relationship between men and women, too, completely diverges from their human nature.

This means that neither the woman sees herself as an equal human being nor does the man view her as such.

The end result of this point of view is to assign *a priori* value and precedence to the genetic and hereditary characteristics of human beings, such as gender, physical appearance, race, ethnicity or language. This is tantamount to surrendering to blind fate. In contrast, in our view, a person's humanity and character is cultivated and fostered through his or her own choices and actions.

Whenever a human being succeeds in pushing aside such social and historical arrangements, freedom, in the true sense of the word, would be given to all regardless of gender.

We recognized that a gender-based ideology, the mullahs' reactionary view towards human beings, is a roadblock and an obstacle to the flourishing of his or her capabilities. As soon as this barrier was pushed aside through a collective and arduous struggle, women began to chide passivity and evasion of responsibility, and instead started to embrace responsibility, accepting key roles in all levels of the movement. Subsequently, the men were able to shed any remnants of the reactionary mindset and attitudes towards women and became advocates of the cause of equality in practice and in deed.

Women must pay the price of their freedom, emancipation and believing in themselves. This would subsequently pave the way for men changing and becoming liberated as well.

Yes, it was this revolt against a reactionary outlook and a rebellion against the enslaving arrangements that unleashed the explosive human energies in the movement. It is a parallel to the idea of converting matter to energy as formulated in Einstein's $E=MC^2$. This unleashed energy is the source of this movement's perseverance against the inhumane regime ruling Iran.

This process has been the greatest experience of my life. It has confirmed my thinking on the nature of human beings in practice, proving that every individual has the capability to summon and revive their true human essence. This has tremendously strengthened my hope and belief in the possibility of changing human beings for the better.

Such an outlook on human beings finds one of its manifestations in the mantra "We can and we must." It means that a human being must develop into what he or she is capable of becoming. It means that there is a vast hidden sea of capabilities in every human being that can make possible what may seem impossible.

AN ENORMOUS TRANSFORMATION

The most significant achievement of this transformation has been the women assuming responsibilities and establishing their hegemony on a large scale and not simply in isolated cases.

Our experience made it palpably clear that defeating the curse of inequality is impossible without first taking a leap; leadership responsibilities must be given to the most competent women without the slightest degree of anxiety.

Women's assumption of leadership positions brought about a major transformation throughout our movement. For women in particular, it served as an important springboard. The organization's 1985 report indicated that the percentage of women in the central council rose from 15 to 34 percent, a growth of 200 percent. In this way, the impasse on women accepting such responsibilities had been overcome. However, this was only the beginning.

This leap forward and the new environment that it created in the organization allowed us to carry out a profound revolution in everyone's outlook, but we did not intend to stop there. The movement's primary goals, democracy and progress, had become intertwined with the drive to emancipate women. We were a movement that believed body and soul that any progress and development depended on the women's activism. Therefore, we were poised to move toward the total rejection of male-dominated culture. The precondition for this, of course, was a revolution in our way of thinking.

As women gradually occupied key positions at the top, their male subordinates felt as if their world was shrinking. It was difficult for them to believe in women, and their hidden resistance revealed itself in a lack of interest in their responsibilities.

It took me several years and thousands of hours of discussions, in both small and large groups, to encourage these women and men, all of whom believed in equality in principle, to step into this new world not only in theory but in practice, too. Indeed, to abolish the double oppression, you must double your efforts.

While going through a gradual and practical path of development, our movement began to see the fruits of its labor in practice and went forward step by step. I regularly convened meetings to examine individual problems. The officials in charge of each section or department followed up after these meetings. Three years later, the proportion of women to men in the National Liberation Army's general command staff had topped 50%, as 7 of the 15 members of the general command were women.

Meanwhile, the misogynous mullahs closely followed these internal developments and the growing status of our women. Alarmed, they tried in vain to slander our movement, accusing us of all sorts of sexual corruption. The mullahs were deeply terrified of the impact of this movement on women in Iran and the escalation of their resistance. In 1988, one of the suppressive organs of the regime called the "Central Komiteh" admitted in an internal report to Khomeini that our revolutionary emancipation of women had in fact strengthened and expanded our movement while serving as a major inspiration for Iranian women. According to this report, "The Mojahedin's internal revolution has become a means of proving the organization's promotion of equal rights for women and men and it has resulted in more female sympathizers being attracted to the organization." Elsewhere it noted: "They used appealing methods, mixed them with practical application and examples, and achieved their objectives."

We organized our movement in a way that allowed women to enter all of the areas, departments and fields that were traditionally reserved for men, giving them access and opportunities to the relevant expertise and qualifications required. Women began to participate in large numbers in military matters through their involvement in the National Liberation Army (NLA). First, they conquered the most masculine types of work and received training up to the level of commanders. Simultaneously, their sisters began to move up the ranks of responsibility in executive management and political affairs.

From 1988 to 1993, the equality movement took major steps forward. New values and views of women began to influence the entire movement. As these qualified women began to directly affect the everyday affairs of each department, I began receiving daily reports from men, underlining the serious and effective impact of women's role. Indeed, those who had taken part in this transformation were compelled to forget their old value system. All eyes were gradually opened to a new reality. The most prominent feature that had the most significant impact on the work environment was, first and foremost, these women's extreme sense of responsibility, particularly in the sensitive military field. They demonstrated a maximum willingness to learn, displayed extraordinary discipline, decisiveness, and most important of all, a selfless devotion and committed relationships. As such, the work environment was filled with compassion and deep human sentiments.

We had begun our combat organization with independent all-women battalions, but soon merged them into mixed units for a harmonious structure. Beyond the many values brought to life in this revolution of minds, I must recall the role that these women – who at the time comprised 50% of the executive committee and 50% of the overall command of the NLA – played in keeping healthy relationships between the sexes. This allowed us to create a completely mixed army, which challenged the enemy with extremely high combat capabilities. When women's concealed energies are set free, they demonstrate their constructive role in emancipating men. These women's methods of collective teamwork allowed them to increase efficiency, strengthen humane relationships and establish the most appropriate modus operandi in order to make the best use of their experience and training.

Moving at a remarkable pace, we reached a turning point. Our whole apparatus of both men and women was ready for another leap forward. At this stage, we adopted a policy of positive discrimination and female leadership to rid our movement of the last vestiges of male-dominant tendencies and lead the way to the final stage of gender equality. Of the more valuable achievements of this era were the new contexts for relationships among women themselves. Before anything else, these women had to love their sisters and show solidarity in their efforts. Such relationships could be realized only when these women truly believed in one another and mutually accepted women commanding women. I think you will concur that this marks the beginning of a mature relationship among human beings.

In 1993, all members and candidates for membership in the PMOI leadership council elected by the Mojahedin's central council were women.

THE CHALLENGE OF DISBELIEF

Traveling on this road was by no means easy. At every stage we had to grapple with numerous issues. Before anything else, let us point to some of the psychological obstacles we had to endure on this path. As the famous Russian writer Leo Tolstoy said, "We must speak of things that every one knows but no one has the power to express."

Women's main obstacle is a destructive mentality about themselves. This is a deep-rooted problem called disbelief, an absence of belief in their own capability to assume key positions. Such disbelief existed both in men and women and it was the principal challenge that every man and woman had to first overcome.

The men used to think: Why should men, who have gained so many years of experience, work under the hegemony of women? Could women handle matters requiring the hard work that had always been handled by competent and experienced men with experience in the struggle against the mullahs? Equality is good but not in all realms. Such was the reaction from the men.

The greater problem, however, was women's disbelief in themselves. Most of them said: Could we undertake such jobs? Will anyone respect us? Everyone looks at us as if our responsibilities are superficial and that there are other people behind the scene who actually lead and run affairs. These concerns made women feel anxious and prevented them from having the necessary confidence to take risks at work.

There were many examples where women lost their self-confidence following the first mistake they made at work and subsequently withdrew from that position of responsibility. Sometimes, women in high positions became passive for a long time after a failure and did not accept any further serious responsibilities. If they did, they remained very shaky. They would cry or become downtrodden when encountering a difficulty. They became depressed and did not stay in the field and if they did stay, they were passive inside and avoided solving problems. Every single one of our women has experienced situations like this and there are many examples in this regard.

Every woman had to come to the realization that she should discard notions of herself as being second-class, weak, phony or an irresponsible person. However, she should never succumb to such views. Women had to instead learn that only the ideals of freedom and emancipation should guide their actions because this is the imperative for their people and country.

Therefore, every woman must be guided by the approach and views of those who ask them to hold on to their positions and fight every weakness and stroke of male-dominated culture. There is an incessant fight occurring between these two opposing feelings inside every woman and it serves as a guide for action for all women in difficult circumstances.

Every woman has had to answer this question: What is important in the long run? The genuine obstacles in one's mind or one's commitment to the cause of every human being and the relationship everyone would establish with the outside to strengthen their commitment to their cause.

DEFYING THE OBJECTIFICATION OF WOMEN

A woman's physical makeup is a colossal problem that enslaves them to such an extent that every woman is worried about changes in her appearance from the day she is born until the day she dies. She is worried about aging, the appearance of a single gray hair or wrinkles on her skin. These are constant concerns and she is always upset about them, finding throughout life that she is broken inside. She sees herself as nothing more than a commodity. These are the symptoms of viewing women as objects or commodities. But when the same woman rids herself of these perceptions, heavy chains fall from her hands and feet and she becomes liberated. We have many rich experiences in this regard. There are many women in our ranks who have overcome this problem and achieved valuable results.

One of these women said: "I was an intelligent, educated and employed woman. Deep down in my mind, however, I believed that the main criterion was a woman's external beauty. I thought that regardless of a woman's level of education or employment, in the end, what dictates her position in society is her outward appearance. Even after I became politically active and joined the National Liberation Army, I could not believe what I had heard about NLA women in positions of command until I saw it with my own eyes. Before that, I used to think that whatever was being said in this regard only served propaganda purposes and in reality, women could not have anything more than a mere formal role. So, I set out to find the criteria for the promotion and elevation of women there and particularly to see if women who are not especially pretty could hold positions of high responsibility and command. (Of course, admitting to harboring such thoughts was very difficult for progressive women who are engaged in political struggle). I was amazed at myself. As an intellectual woman, I wondered why women's beauty was so important to me despite my experiences as an intellectual. I was astonished to see with my own eyes that beauty was not the criterion of worth and that the road was open to any woman to hold key positions, regardless of her looks. It was at such points that the deep-seated dogmas in my mind shattered and I started to believe that a woman's personality and character is distinct from her physical characteristics."

This is an example of a woman's perspective. But men also had their own experiences. I remember one of them saying: "In the beginning, when we faced a female commander who was not considered beautiful by ordinary social standards, I felt I did not want to accept her hegemony. I thought, 'Why should I accept her authority?' Granted, although I had accepted to have a female superior, why should I be so humiliated to be bossed around by someone who is considered to be at the lowest levels (by our previous standards)?" Of course it was very difficult for men to admit to harboring such thoughts.

Another teary-eyed man said: "These thoughts struck my mind as fast as lightning, but when I started to analyze them at a deeper level, I began to identify the effects of the male-dominated culture with its inhuman and misogynic foundations. How was it that in dealing with a woman, before focusing on her personality and her capabilities as a human being, men focused on her external appearance and equated her identity with that appearance? ... This was where I and other men started to resent the culture that was so deeply rooted in our minds. We decided to fight this culture even more vigorously... It was at this point that we grasped the real value of women accepting responsibility in our movement and understood how greatly it helps men in dispensing with male-dominated values."

Women's hegemony

In its efforts to promote equality within its ranks, the Iranian resistance realized that, before anything else, we must ask women to undertake in their share of responsibilities. At the same time, we must grant the most competent of them positions of leadership and responsibility without any fear or concern because they are capable of conquering any challenges. Otherwise, it would be impossible for women to prove their competence by relying on a classical approach within the paradigm of a male-dominated regime.

With the gradual assumption of responsibilities by women, new values began to appear in all areas of women's activities. Men were also actively and most admirably engaged in this developing trend. They had clearly understood that this is the inevitable path to free their people, their country and themselves. In fact, they blazed the trail and took huge strides.

The resistance subsequently reached a turning point. At this stage, all men and women of the movement were ready to take a new leap forward. This is when we launched the policy of positive discrimination and hegemony of women to remove all traces of male-dominated culture and cultivate an atmosphere that enabled the maturing of principles of equality.

But men did not simply give up their hegemony and domination over the areas in which they had acquired long years of experience. But neither did women take on the new demanding responsibilities and enforce their hegemony and command as they should have.

It was difficult for women to accept the responsibility of command, even at low levels. A PMOI woman said: "I had just adapted myself to a certain extent to accept difficult responsibilities and jobs that men had so far monopolized. I had managed to work with armored vehicles and drive and repair them. Suddenly, I faced a new problem when I was told to command a number of men. I felt I did not have the power to do so. Accepting this responsibility was so difficult that I could not sleep at nights. I asked God, 'How could I order those who are older and more experienced?' I remember the first night I went to my superior and cried and asked her not to demand such a responsibility from me. She asked 'Why?' I said, 'From the bottom of my heart, I do not want my weaknesses and inabilities to surface in front of men. If I make a mistake, I will lose all credit and I will never be able to hold my head up. How could I be the commander of so many men who are older than me? I feel powerless in enforcing this new hegemony on them.' "

"My superior promised to help me at every turn. So by relying on her and based on the commitment I had made to embrace any difficulty in the path of the struggle, I asked myself, 'Should I not be prepared to overcome all the hardships in order to free my country from the mullahs' oppressive and criminal regime? Should I not get rid of all forms of the misogynist ideology in my own mind in order to advance this struggle?' I figured that without stepping on this path, it was impossible to run the affairs of the movement and achieve the desired outcome. This is how I decided to engage in a difficult struggle with the misogynist culture and ideology in my mind. Then, I vowed to myself not to cower in the face of any pressures I would encounter in this path but instead welcome them with open arms."

This was an example of the problems our politically active women faced when trying to establish their hegemony over men. In practice, however, we saw that establishing women's hegemony over women was not an easy task either and bore numerous complexities. Regarding this, one of the women in the resistance said, "Establishing command and hegemony over women was very difficult for me. I thought it was even more difficult than commanding men."

Another said, "When I became the commander of a number of women, I suddenly encountered various hidden feelings inside myself that I was not previously familiar with… Initially I constantly compared myself with them, and had deep-seated feelings of jealousy and envy, which were torturous to describe and admit to. I asked myself, 'As a woman involved in political struggle, a woman seeking equality and as a revolutionary and responsible woman, how could I envy the women under my command? How could I be jealous of them because they were younger and more beautiful or more educated, more capable, more artistically inclined, or more capable of adapting themselves?' "

"I realized that if I did not turn this feeling of jealousy into a sense of love for them, I would not be competent to command them. Then again, I thought that I could not resolve this problem within myself. If everything began and ended within the confines of my mind and heart, then I would have preferred not to be in this position in the first place. But I remembered that I had made a commitment to struggle for freedom, to rid my country of tyranny and oppression. I remembered that women's freedom and emancipation were indispensable to my people's freedom. It was such an understanding that propelled me forward and helped me overcome my negative feelings and tendencies. In contrast to my earlier reactions, now I could feel compassion towards other women, appreciate their beauty and suffer with them when they were suffering. I felt overjoyed about being united with them and seeing their beauties and capabilities.

After a while I found out that their beauty or lack thereof did no longer bother me. These characteristics lost their influence and what mattered was the beauty of their human personality, their thinking, their freedom and their responsibility, and not how they looked... Later, I felt I loved my fellow female combatants like my own sisters. All of them looked lovely and beautiful to the same extent, despite their different physical appearances. This was an incredibly uplifting experience that I would never exchange for anything else in the world."

"It was at this point that I also tamed the monster of my own mind's obsession with appearance. As a woman, I was no longer concerned about a lock of grey hair, or a wrinkle appearing on my face or about growing one year older and feeling useless. I think this is an enduring pain that every woman suffers from the time she is born, an agony that crushes a woman at every moment of her life and drives her out of the ordinary cycle of human life because she has been forced to see herself as a commodity. Indeed, if every morning a woman were to get up and decide that instead of worrying about how she looks for work that day, she would think about how to be more responsible, a better human being and free to undertake further responsibilities. Imagine what a comfortable and greater world she would create for herself and others. In this way, women can be free from the chains hiding within them.

"This is the requirement for the world of freedom and emancipation of women and all human beings. Instead of competing with one another, people are friends, sisters, mothers, companions and supporters of one another. Instead of feeling humiliated and envying or obstructing the other's growth and promotion, they could enjoy each other's achievements."

This is one of the most remarkable discussions that the Iranian resistance movement has been involved in. Many women initially did not have faith in it. The first time they encountered such challenges, they said we set aside the negative values when we chose to engage in political struggle. This was why we could step onto this path. How could such challenges re-emerge? They were right. They had set aside the old negative values in the first phase of struggle, but those values remained deep down in their minds and needed to be completely eradicated.

NEW RELATIONS AMONG WOMEN

Relations among women are generally, and on many occasions, character- ized by rivalry and competition. They find their space encroached upon. Women feel threatened by the progress of other women. Women's hege- mony could compensate for centuries of male-dominated culture, which prevented the possibility for women to develop and then ex- ercise their abilities to lead.

As a result of this campaign, women succeeded in adopting noble values and rose above a decadent and reactionary culture.

As a first accomplishment, they came to believe in themselves and their capabilities. When they discovered how necessary their roles were in the advancement of the struggle against religious tyranny, they decided to leave behind the world of irresponsibility and pas- sivity, where a women's identity is reliant on others. Instead, they stepped into a realm of responsible women who led a struggle with all its potential consequences.

They parted with vices that would hold them back, like jealousy, judgment and attributing worth to physical characteristics, appear- ances, and age, all of which greatly deplete women's energies. They also managed to replace attitudes of frailty and fragility with a sense of forte and strength.

They shed their fears of experiencing defeat or exhibiting weakness in the face of difficulties. Instead of succumbing to pressure, they learned to cultivate the power within themselves to overcome defeat.

Instead of losing hope, they learned to remain helpful and assiduous in opening the path to victory.

In our movement, relations among women have changed in a way that women stand alongside each other and support and hear one another as if they were biological sisters. They fulfill the most cumbersome responsibilities collectively and on the basis of these relations. They do not undermine each other. Progress made by any one of them is a source of encouragement and inspiration for other women. Furthermore, collective effort used to elevate the responsibilities of other women is considered a virtue.

Each woman in the resistance has come to the realization that by cooperating with and supporting her colleagues, she can actually empower herself. On this path, they have attained an incredible ability to make sacrifices for their sisters.

Therefore, in the resistance, women all help each other in the undertaking of more and more responsibilities. Their cooperation and support for one another is remarkable and considered a "new creation."

Each woman in this movement believes that by supporting and cooperating with other women, she becomes more empowered herself. The path for the blossoming and progression of every woman is contingent upon the growing number of women she helps reach their common goal and fulfill their responsibilities. Indeed, this is a new world that is entirely different from women's past history.

EMANCIPATION OF MEN

The aim of the internal transformation was not simply to switch the places of men and women and compete against the existing model. It was to form relations based on freedom, equality and democracy. That is why I have to tell you that among the other achievements of this transformation were the rise of a generation of liberated men who were committed to the cause of gender equality. There are light years of distance separating these men from the archaic and exploitative "values" of a patriarchal society, including an inclination to dominate others and seek hegemony.

And in their belief in equality and in their attitude towards women, they have reached new heights of purity and a blossoming of their human essence. They have liberated themselves of the desire to selfishly compete, to harbor personal ambitions, to be close-minded and to eliminate others. They have gained true and enriched self-confidence. They have thus far taken this difficult journey with the help of their own volition and iron resolve.

I am pleased to say that in light of these relations that are devoid of oppression and exploitation, members of the Iranian resistance have been able to elevate their abilities to engage in collective work to the next level.

I must emphasize that active work and participation alongside one colleague is, on the one hand, the basis of a democratic order in one's relationship, and on the other hand, a determining factor for success in all endeavors.

The women and men of this resistance have shunned the destructive attitude of "first for me," and instead always give priority to their colleagues. In other words, through sacrifice, they have succeeded in reaching new heights in mutual group work. This is the result of resisting against the eccentricity that stunts the growth of people as human beings.

This transformation has helped both women and men flourish and become affable, and to constantly strengthen their resolve and motivation. It has also instilled compassion and forgiveness, in contrast to the reactionaries' cold-heartedness and vengeance.

Doubtless, we have perhaps just passed the halfway mark. But we will continue to move ahead until the mullahs are overthrown and until we have utilized all of our accomplishments in tomorrow's free Iran.

There is another area where members of the resistance movement fought against the ideology of gender apartheid.

A male member of the resistance noted, "I had come to accept the notion of women's promotion and their undertaking of responsibilities in a few instances and I was happy with myself that I was able to do so. But hearing about the formation of an all-woman leadership council sent a sudden shock through my body. I felt nothing had been left for me to achieve. The ideology of male domination could not accept women taking hold of all affairs while still expecting everything to go well."

"But I soon realized that this was reactionary ideology based on gender apartheid which was operating deep down in my mind. For me, it was challenging to fight. Unfortunately, the old ideology, with its long history, was deeply entrenched in my mind. It was as if it merely withdrew every time the new values launched an offensive, but later emerged from a new hiding place and resumed its fight."

"For example, whenever I encountered a mistake committed by my female commander, I referred to a higher superior and complained about the mistake while emphasizing the general faults of my direct commander. Of course, at the time, I did not really think about what I was doing. I thought I was simply reacting to one of my natural and democratic rights in the organization by expressing the criticisms I had about my commander. When I finished talking, the higher commander told me, 'OK, fine, you are right. But is this criticism aimed at improving the actions of your commander or are you saying that she is not competent and should be removed from her current position? Or do you want your responsibilities changed so that you could be at ease?' "

"I went back and reflected on the episode responsibly, and I concluded that it is not the case that she is incompetent. When I realized the hidden agenda behind my actions, I became embarrassed and immediately afterwards, I remembered what I had been taught. I accepted my mistake in order to rid myself of the shame. Indeed, all the values of the male-dominated ideology in my mind directed me to resist the new phenomenon of women's hegemony by scrutinizing every little detail and by coming up with excuses that would allow me to refuse bowing to this trend. Once I exposed these thoughts, I decided to fight the male-dominated culture instead of submitting to it."

One of the other women also said, "When I heard about the formation of an all-woman leadership council, I said, 'Oh God, what will happen to the serious responsibilities?' Are we going to leave the destiny of our movement in the hands of a group of women? Is this even possible? Granted that so far, these women have made a lot of achievements, but is it prudent to give them all the major responsibilities? What happens if we fail?"

Moving from surface to depth

It was not until after women's hegemony became fully ingrained in the resistance movement that the serious and profound struggle against the culture of male-domination began to take shape. This is because deep-rooted opposition to the new culture gave rise to a series of obstacles.

For example, after successfully going through the period of accepting key responsibilities, women began limiting their responsibilities to management, coordination and general administrative activities. But when it came to deeper problems, such as the resolution of existing issues and challenges, they left things completely up to the men under their command. At the outset, this seemed to them to be very normal and justified. They asked themselves, "What's the problem? We are managing and employing their abilities. This is what counts and it will suffice."

It took a long time before women realized that this rationale stemmed from male-dominated culture where women fear getting involved with substantial issues of responsibilities. When women learned that in order to become substantially involved in their work, they must not just count on men but must also take other women like themselves seriously, it became essential for responsible women to work with their fellow sisters to engage on a more serious level with their work. It was valuable to both bring themselves into a deeper level of involvement and to also help support and guide other women, to take them seriously and to encourage them to fight their self doubts.

They also reached another very important conclusion that in this new world, they needed to train men to develop the same characteristics. As such, every woman in a position of responsibility took another major stride in overcoming her own and other women's disbeliefs. They gradually proceeded in the struggle by rejecting the culture that was dominated by males and which considered women weak.

FIGHTING MALE DOMINATION IN THE DEPTHS

Because the fight over hegemony was, at its root, a struggle against male domination, men also struggled in confronting the paradigm shift. They had to come to terms with women's equality and hegemony in a substantive way. Women in high positions of responsibility and command faced serious resistance by men when they sought to get involved in the fundamentals of their work.

Men argued that since they had already accepted women as commanders, they shouldn't try to overreach into other areas of men's expertise. At first, men were antagonistic. Sometimes, it was not just dialogue and argument, but quarrelling and bickering. Subsequently, after learning that this was a reaction caused by the remnants of male-dominated culture, albeit under the guise of logical reasoning, they began to fight it on their own.

Later, once hostile reactions subsided and were overcome, passivism began to emerge. While men had openly agreed not to put up boundaries around their areas of expertise and recognize women's involvement, the difficulty of accepting this caused some to withdraw and become passive. This was a reaction that we absolutely did not want to take place, so we combated it. Later, men discovered for themselves that this was another reaction resulting from the same culture of male domination. They subsequently realized that not only did they have to let their female superiors get involved in their area of expertise but that they had to remain active throughout this process.

This was one of the most crucial turning points in the men's struggle against male-dominated culture. They learned how to open up their once-exclusive areas of responsibility and began to include others. This was one of the most difficult achievements for the men of the movement, but they succeeded.

The advancement of the cause of equality must never mean passivism or withdrawal for men. On the contrary, an indication of success in this process would be the emergence of men who are more serious, responsible and active than before. It should be stressed that the marker of success in men's fight against the culture of gender apartheid and male domination is that, like women, they also tap into the enormous amount of energy that was previously wasted by submitting to a male-dominated culture. This is how men would come to feel free and become more responsible. Therefore, this is a revolution for both women and men equally that enables them to become more responsible. It does not imply the arrival of one and the departure of another. From the outset, the goal of this movement has and continues to be to help and empower them to fulfill their responsibilities in a better manner than in the past.

SEEING THE POSITIVE SIDE

The experience of the Iranian resistance has shown that new and more humane values were created when a generation of women assumed roles in leadership. This was not only a guarantee for women's equality, but also a process that emancipated both women and men by eliminating self-alienation, thus providing the opportunity to realize their true human nature and achieve unity and excellence.

The fact that a pioneering generation of men and women voluntarily and consciously chose leaders from among people who had been historically deprived of equal status as human beings, shows a transition from the male-dominated world and backward values to a more humane one. This is actually a cultural change that helps the essence within people blossom. Men and women of this movement have proudly passed the great test of making this choice and have remained steadfast on this path for many years. By swimming

111

against the predominant current of history, they have rejected the thousands-year-old culture of gender apartheid and exploitation.

One of the most important results of traveling on this path is that (as the Quran says) people can see with their hearts through the humanization of their senses. They can see and understand the goodness, purity and what is called the compassion and kindness of God. In this kind of a world, it is not the shortcomings or deficiencies of humans that are primary or essential, but rather the relationships of every human being with their own kind and colleagues as well as the degree to which they are prepared to make sacrifices for one another.

Indeed, if we accept that humankind is an extraordinary gem and the unique essence of nature and history, then our outlook towards humankind should embody this.

TRANSFORMATION OF CULTURE

The complicated and long-standing social and cultural issues resolved by our movement in its quest for gender equality could be the subject of extensive discussions A cursory review of this point follows.

The women of the Iranian resistance movement, regardless of their social status or class, enjoy, on a scale of thousands and in a systematic way, a new quality of strength in their personalities. Women's historically-defined weaknesses have been eradicated: fragility, instability, jealousy, rivalry, fear of socialization, dreading to express oneself in a social context, fear of accepting responsibility, and avoiding to assume responsibilities traditionally dominated by men or fearing to impose hegemony over men.

All those passive, silent, secluded women have instead become active, strong and capable, and have formed new qualities when it comes to loving others and expressing the highest level of human emotions. As for the undertaking of responsibilities, they boldly take risks and if they commit any mistakes or fail, they do not lose confidence.

These women are empowered to accept more responsibilities and maintain their hegemony. Their prominent characteristic is their liberation from exploitative chains and limitations. Of course, all this has become possible because they have chosen to pursue a grand human ideal. In this process, the men of the movement have also traversed a very long and arduous path alongside women. This path has emancipated men from the chains of male-domination, turning them into humans who, before all else, see their own humanity as contingent upon women's equality.

Our generation is overjoyed and proud to have gone through such a great experience and to be able to share its achievements with the movement for emancipation and the abolition of gender discrimination and apartheid. This is the experience of teaching, training and educating a generation of women and men who, in their struggle against the culture of male domination, have overcome challenges that had seemed insurmountable in the course of this struggle.

The men have become some of the most ardent advocates of women's rights and have proven this in practice. They have witnessed firsthand women assuming responsibilities.

I wish I were a proficient writer, a capable poet or a skillful painter in order to portray the epic struggle that is being waged by the Iranian resistance movement. History will certainly do so. Numerous books, the most beautiful poems and some of the most exquisite paintings could be created to depict the movement and every one of its heroes and heroines.

At the same time, beyond all the suffering and torture, the potentials and the magnificence of nature's creation of women and men who have been freed from the bondage of gender apartheid are bountiful. Sadly, gender-based cultures and ideologies have prevented these powers and beauties from being fully realized.

By seeing the epics created in the Iranian resistance by these women and the men who follow them, I thank God for creating me as a human being and as a woman and giving us this power to be able to struggle and embark on the journey towards emancipation.

7

Power for Democratic Change

The Iranian resistance has the necessary social and political where-withal to bring about democratic change. Most importantly, it relies on a broad social base of support and has 3,400 resistance activists in camps Ashraf and Liberty in Iraq, many of whom have been engaged in the resistance for freedom for nearly three decades. The movement is also very well organized and relies on a legitimate and progressive ideology. Still, it is women's leadership that remains as the underlying spirit that materializes all this support.

Owing to being exploited and oppressed for centuries, women are highly tolerant and motivated during the struggle in order to swiftly compensate for these past wrongdoings. In the course of confronting the clerical regime, we saw that women were full of potential energy, much like very compressed springs. Once they found the opportunity to break free from the chains of discrimination and to assume responsibilities, they had a tendency to advance by leaps and bounds.

Women's widespread and heroic participation in the efforts to confront the clerical dictatorship during the 1979 anti-monarchic revolution, which included their laudable resistance under torture, proves that they are a flourishing force. On a macro-social level, this force advances democratic change in Iran and fuels the struggle for liberation. It is, therefore, the fundamental pillar and bedrock of the Iranian resistance's power.

Women's active participation in leadership and the solution that they offer also turns men into a force for change. The solution offered by women's participation amounts to breaking the chains of exploitation that limit hearts and minds. That is why men, who are alienated from their true human essence because of the culture of male-domination, rediscover their true human essence. This transformation can be regarded as a genuine awakening or a real change of culture, and it is the trigger that sets off the eruption of hidden energies and potentials.

GUARANTEE OF DEMOCRACY

How does the decisive and determining role of women guarantee democracy?

Women's active and equal participation in political leadership makes possible the formation of democratic potentials in government or in the alternative force. Otherwise, the restrictions and barriers existing on their path to undertaking their political role would not only violate their democratic rights but would also damage and impair the very foundations of democracy itself. This is because democracy in its most fundamental sense relies on human rights.

Democracy, in the sense of political rights, cannot solely be enjoyed by males and must not allow any room for discrimination. When half of the population in a society (women) is denied an equal share in power, democracy in the remaining half (among men) is either non-existent or, at best, fragile and unstable. The truth of this argument might be better seen after a closer examination of societies around the world today. Such a study would reveal that the scale of women's participation in political leadership is the true measure of democratic progress in a particular society. When women's active participation and leadership roles are prominent, tyrannical relations based on a male-dominated culture are bound to subside.

The notion of women's participation in leadership is a novel outlook and a new approach that inherently advocates respecting people instead of humiliating them. It also emphasizes positive traits and human abilities instead of negative characteristics and weaknesses, relying on love instead of hate, and on collective efforts instead of isolated individual activities. All these factors provide the necessary ingredients for democracy and mutual understanding in political life.

THE ROLE OF WOMEN'S LEADERSHIP IN ECONOMIC PROGRESS

Women's participation in political leadership plays a vital role in economic development. Today, putting more power in the hands of women is described as "the engine for human development."[1] Recent initiatives have failed in many respects, particularly in that they have failed to improve the general conditions of society and have exacerbated the poverty rate in developing nations. Of course, the main victims of poverty are women everywhere. According to the World Bank, women represent 40% of the world's labor force but hold just one percent of the world's total wealth.[2] Standards such as government transparency and accountability, as well as the efficiency of government services have plummeted. Meanwhile, rates of violence, corruption and lawlessness have risen dramatically.

The fact is that under the current circumstances, where a devastating imbalance of power works against women, the prevailing forms of

---

1. The United Nations Development Programme report, "Women's Participation as the Engine of Human Development," November 14, 2011.

2. The World Bank, The World Development Report 2012: Gender Equality and Development, released on September 18, 2011.

development, too, originate from the outlook and methods established by tyranny, corruption and the squandering of human and material resources. The way out of this situation lies in the recognition of women's role. This recognition and utilization of women's potential would not only help the progress of all humankind, but it would also remove the obstacles and chains that are created by a male-dominated culture.

Promoting gender equality, considered a human right, is at the heart of the United Nations Third Millennium Development Goals. The platform stresses that having an equal voice in political decision-making, from the family to the highest levels of government, is a key element in the empowerment of women.[3]

In the 1990s, some of the world's greatest economists stepped forward and reiterated that economic development requires freedom. They also asserted, "Nothing, arguably, is as important today in the political economy of development as an adequate recognition of political, economic and social participation and leadership of women."[4]

GROWING INTENSITY OF THE STRUGGLE

The conclusions offered here regarding the effects of women's active and equal participation are not founded on a purely theoretical appraisal of the current situation. Rather, they speak to a reality we discovered in the course of the resistance movement's struggle against the ruling mullahs in Iran.

---

3. The United Nations Millennium Development Goals (MDGs) are eight international dvelopment goals that, following the adoption of the UN Millennium Declaration, form a blueprint agreed to by the world's countries and the world's leading development institutions. One of the goals is "promoting gender equality and empowering women."

4. Amartya Sen, *Development as Freedom,* Oxford University Press, 1999, p. 203. Amartya Sen won the 1998 Nobel Prize in Economic Sciences.

In the course of the struggle to topple religious tyranny, this movement realized that it was no longer possible to remove the emerging obstacles on the path to democracy and freedom by relying on the motivations and dynamism of the past century. The political and international circumstances had created restrictions and limitations that required the movement to engage in a more intense struggle and a pay a higher price for not only its advancement, but also its very survival. We recognized that the resistance movement needed to elevate its ideals and thinking. Thus, we found the role of women in leadership to be imperative.

Women's participation in leadership proved to be an effective answer to the question of democratic change in Iran. It became the source of a major cultural transformation in the ranks of our resistance. Some of the experiences in this regard have already been shared with the reader in the previous chapters. But if one were to offer a condensed account of this process, one would only have to say that the history of the advancement of women and their assumption of key positions in our resistance is precisely the history of the intensification of our struggle against the religious tyranny and the fundamentalists ruling Iran.

Since the beginning of this transformation, we have come across several critical junctures where we had to make definitive choices. We either had to abandon the ideals of freedom, democracy and liberation of the Iranian people, or we had to make a decision to sacrifice even more than we already had and wage a more determined struggle to preserve and advance the movement.

With every choice we made, it became more evident that success in our path demanded more dedication and effort and could only be realized through active and equal participation of women. In other words, the ultimate philosophy of that internal transformation that permeated the rank and file of the movement and evolved at every stage since 1985, is achieving democracy and freedom that is made possible through the participation of women in leadership.

Contemporary political and economic developments in other countries also attest to this fact. Instead of out-dated solutions, the substantive involvement of women offers novel answers.

A PROGRESSIVE IDEOLOGY

What does it mean for women to play an active and equal role in leadership?

In addition to occupying managerial positions, this also means parting with the male-dominated ideology, its methods of work and replacing its values with new and more humane ones. To help explain the profound differences among various solutions, the example of the Iranian crisis was presented here, which is a very critical issue in the world today. On the one hand, all proposed solutions, whether based on appeasement or on war and foreign intervention, lead to an impasse and a gloomy outlook as if there were no alternatives. That is to say, if we refuse to accept the status quo–a tyrannical, backward and barbaric fundamentalist regime–then we are left with no other choice but going to war. We reject this notion of *fait accompli*. We have not and will not accept being confined to solutions and paradigms that offer no hope for human liberty. Proposals and strategies that stem from the exploitative mindset cannot offer a way out of this dilemma. However, the thinking that evolves from women's leadership cultivates and fosters the true potentials of humanity and opens up countless doors.

The notion of leadership we are referring to is the result of the flourishing of humane potentials and focuses on humane relations. This represents a great rebellion against male domination and the regressive culture that must be rejected. For this reason, when women assumed leadership positions in our movement, it was not merely a change of management. The goal was to eliminate the foundations of gender apartheid. Men did not leave their posts to be replaced by women who continued to retain and preserve the same relations and same modes of work. Women did not walk in men's footsteps. They had not joined the men's club. The main issue was and remains to replace the obsolete relations based on a male-dominated culture with new humane relations.

Women's presence in the leadership of our resistance did not result in the undermining or disposal of men nor did it make them passive. On the contrary, it liberated them from the shackles of a male-dominated culture that had enslaved their minds, emotions and willpower. They shared their experiences with women and subsequently learned a great deal from those who had conquered new horizons of their own. So, we view women's leadership as a progressive human ideal. In this way, a new set of relationships based on equality, with women taking responsibility and assuming the leadership, has become a possibility.

These sets of relationships, free of exploitation, enable women to express their human character.

These relationships are based on self-sacrifice, giving priority to other's interests over one's own interests and making up for the weaknesses and shortcomings of others; a set of relationships based on active outreach to others, which elevates human beings to their greatest human asset.

Such humanity has enabled the women in the resistance to withstand the highest pressures and most difficult circumstances, not to feel despondent and desperate and not to become passive.

To the contrary, the greater the difficulties and the harder the conditions became, the greater the effort undertaken by the women in the resistance in opening the way and advancing forward.

This has given women such faith that they do not look to chance, or the will of this or that power. Instead of becoming hopeless and desperate, they rely on their own power and on the power of solidarity with their own people in order to further step up their struggle.

Indeed, not surrendering, not giving up, not being content, taking risks, failing time after time, but rising up again, constantly yearning for new ways and ideas, discovering and realizing the slightest human attribute and demonstrating tolerance are what characterize women.

These are the sources of what can be done in the face of what must be done.

OPTIONS FOR CONFRONTING FUNDAMENTALISTS

How to confront fundamentalists is an issue that should concern all advocates of peace and human rights, particularly activists in the equality movement. This is especially so because the threat of Islamic fundamentalism is not solely confined to the Middle East and Islamic countries, but is a specter that plagues Western countries as well.

Determining a prudent policy for confronting Islamic fundamentalism around the globe is directly tied to the policy of confronting the clerical regime of Iran because it is an epicenter of exporting fundamentalism. There are usually two options presented in debates about dealing with this growing threat. One is to appease the clerical regime with the goal of containing and gradually changing it. This is the policy that Western countries have pursued for the past two decades. The other option is to topple the mullahs by a foreign war similar to what happened in Iraq, a scenario no one really likes to see repeated in Iran.

The ruling mullahs in Tehran and all those who have interests in the status quo argue that war is the prerequisite for any serious change and as such conclude that there is no other option left except appeasement. The Iranian resistance, however, rejects the dichotomy of appeasement or war and instead believes that there is a "Third Option," which is actually the only realistic solution for change. This option proposes change by the Iranian people and the resistance.

In 2004, I personally presented this opinion at the European Parliament.[5] Today, one can point out another important issue that is as vital as the main subject. The crucial nature of this issue can be grasped once we answer the question, "Which particular force can advance the Third Option, the real solution for fighting the fundamentalists?" Furthermore, how will the Third Option triumph and who will bear the burden of realizing it?

Our answer is simple: the decisive defeat of Islamic fundamentalists can be made possible through women's pioneering force. This is why we emphasize the need for women's active and equal participation in political leadership whether in Iran or in other parts of the world. The notion that women's participation in political leadership is the antidote to Islamic fundamentalism comes from the experience of

5. December 15, 2004, speech at the Parliament of Europe: "In facing (the Iranian) challenge, two options have been raised: The make-a-deal approach to the clerical regime with the aim of containing it or inducing gradual change. For the past two decades, Western countries have subscribed to this approach."

"The other option is to overthrow the clerical regime by way of an external war, similar to what occurred in Iraq. No one would want to see this repeated in Iran.

"The Tehran mullahs and those who benefit from the status-quo argue that any serious change necessarily involves a foreign war and there is no option but compromise. Today, however, I have come to say that a third option is within reach: Change by Iranian people and resistance.

"If the foreign obstacles are removed, the Iranian people and resistance have the capacity and ability to bring about change. This is the only way to prevent an external war. Giving concessions to the mullahs is not an alternative to war. No concession is going to dissuade the mullahs from continuing their ominous objectives."

Iran and its resistance, which has continued for years through much suffering and sacrifice.

Any force that is contaminated by even the slightest trace of the mullahs' misogynist ideology, or carries with it the same kind of fundamentalism to varying degrees, cannot be decisive in the fight against the regime and does not turn away from the option of appeasement. Could this resistance have ever been capable of fighting fundamentalism if it had not first eradicated the male-dominated ideology from its thinking? There is an Iranian proverb that says, "The knife doesn't cut its own handle."

Our most basic experience in this era in the struggle against fundamentalism has been the necessity of liberating ourselves from the male-dominated ideology. It would be impossible for the resistance to advance its struggle against Islamic fundamentalism without first eradicating all traces of gender discrimination at all levels, just as it is impossible to liberate women without ridding society of fundamentalism.

Therefore, as far as it relates to the three options mentioned above, the main point is that we are no longer confined to a choice between appeasement and war. At their core, these options have the same nature and essence because they have been formed under the prevailing paradigm. This paradigm can only exist and be bolstered through power, violence and the squandering of enormous opportunities and wealth. It is also at odds with tapping into the never-ending resource of human potential and is unable to remove the obstacles on the path of human progress. When this kind of thinking is put aside, it becomes evident that the forces behind what compelled us to choose between the status quo and war are false. To accept either appeasement or war would be tantamount to submitting to compulsion. The real solution is democratic and humanitarian and is applied through the active participation of women in the leadership of this resistance and through running the affairs of future Iran.

A FOUNDER OF RESISTANCE

Our point of departure in this transformation was to overthrow the religious fascism ruling Iran, but in order to rebuild the free Iran of tomorrow, we must remain armed with this outlook so that we can create democratic institutions in our society. In other words, the Iranian resistance also has the historical responsibility to be a builder and a founder.

If democracy is not built on things such as gender equality, the participation of all people, free choice of all sectors of society and unconditional freedom of speech, then it would quickly deviate and take on reactionary tendencies.

The idea of equality in our movement is inspirational and holds a promise for Iranian society and especially its women and youth.

When you target sexism, you are actually attempting to shatter the cornerstone of the velayat-e faqih system (absolute clerical rule).

When you target the mullahs' misogyny, you are in fact aiming at the heart of their ideology. As a result, neither the mullahs' jurisprudence nor Sharia, nor their reactionary laws and culture can find a solid footing.

This explains why the mullahs target the PMOI incessantly through utter demagoguery. In their view, the PMOI's first offense is its unwavering commitment to bring about regime change in Iran.

But, in addition to this, in accordance with the mullahs' Sharia, the PMOI has committed a cardinal sin because the Iranian resistance believes that Iranian women are competent enough and must assume leadership of the democratic Iran of tomorrow.

According to the regime's Sharia, the PMOI have committed a cardinal sin because, in contrast to the mullahs' reactionary ideology, they believe that men are not intrinsically deprived of will power and are not slaves of their primal instincts. They also believe that the desire to establish supremacy and commit violence against women, considered virtues in the mullahs' religious jurisprudence and Sharia, have no place whatsoever in Islam.

It is due to the committing of such unforgivable sins that, with endless rage and vengeance, the mullahs slander the PMOI and call it a "cult," while continuing to suppress them. For many years, the mullahs have made them the target of a campaign of demonization and misinformation.

It is because this is a movement that completely and absolutely rejects the ruling ideology and behavior and has risen up to overthrow oppression, inequality and injustice in its foundation.

8

Ashraf, A Brilliant Example

"My violin is my weapon against fundamentalism."

My violin is a weapon in my struggle against the fundamentalist regime that bans women from practicing art and whose only aim is to see us drown in hopelessness and despair in Ashraf. The sound of my violin sends our message to the whole world. It was with this motivation that my friends and I began to learn music as novices in Ashraf's school of music. Today, our instructors acknowledge that we have accomplished in just two years what would ordinarily take others five years to accomplish in normal music academies.
– Adeleh Goudarzi

Today, the issue of women and the need for their active participation in all political, social and economic realms has turned into the most urgent imperative for progress, democracy and peace. Without women and the leading role that they play, the struggle for freedom cannot advance. Without their active and equal presence in every level of the decision-making process, democracy would be devoid of its very essence. Furthermore, the spread of poverty, inequality and a waste of human and material resources would take the place of economic development in the absence of women's real and actual involvement.

It is, therefore, necessary to study and analyze the issue of equality itself, the mechanisms of removing the obstacles in its path, the strategy to advance it and successful models and examples. The most recent example in the modern history of Iran and Islam is the three decades of struggle by women in the Iranian resistance and, at its heart, the experiences gained from the steadfastness of the residents of camps Ashraf and Liberty in Iraq.

Ashraf is situated about 70 kilometers from the Iranian border in Iraq. Until 2012, it was home to 3,400 members of the People's Mojahedin Organization of Iran (PMOI/MEK), the strongest and largest organization opposed to the Iranian regime. The PMOI has engaged in struggles against two dictatorships since 1965. In 2012, most of the residents were forcibly moved to Camp Liberty under the pretext of being transferred to third countries, while the real intention was to increase the pressure on them to break their resistance.

Many of the activists residing in Ashraf and Liberty have dedicated between 10 and 25 years of their lives to the struggle for democracy in their homeland. The group has some 1,000 female members and boasts the largest concentration of pioneers of the equality movement in the world. Most of them were either students or are graduates of European, American, Canadian and Iranian universities. Two hundred of them were political prisoners under the clerical regime and spent an average of five years in prison suffering through enormous amounts of pressure and torture. Some of them courageously escaped prison and fled to Ashraf. Still others who were being monitored by the regime also took a great risk by bravely overcoming challenges and going to Ashraf.[1]

---

1. A number of these women have written prison memoirs in recent years, explaining their horrendous ordeals in the prisons of the mullahs' regime.

Women have assumed responsibilities in all realms of activity in Ashraf and are actively engaged in political affairs, education, production, procurement, organization, music orchestras and more. Half the members of Ashraf's Grand Orchestra are women.[2]

---

2. Numerous restrictions and the tightening siege of Ashraf in recent years brought about a situation where few reporters received permission for visit. However, the reporters who were able to visit have often pointed out the role of women in their reports. On March 19, 2005, the Knight Ridder news agency reported:

On one recent night, 300 women from Unit 6 gathered for dinner in a cafeteria where artists practiced for an Iranian New Year gala. The all-female orchestra tuned up with the theme song to the film "The Godfather," followed by a purple-clad singer who stirred the crowd with folk tunes from Iran.

"See?" whispered one young woman called Khojasteh, whose name means "happiness" in Farsi. "Women in Ashraf have so many talents. They can sing, they can play and they can fight."

In the audience were Somayeh, 24, who boasted of her skills with an assault rifle, and Farkhondeh, 28, a tank mechanic who's now in charge of electrical maintenance at the camp. There was Maryam, 39, whose toenails were ripped out during torture in an Iranian prison, and Hajar, 67, whose husband and two sons died fighting for the Mujahedeen. They were all smart, engaging women – and none has left the confines of Ashraf in two years.

The most revered figure of the group as Mahnaz Bazazi, who lost her legs during a U.S. air strike on a Mujahedeen camp during the 2003 invasion. Young women gathered around her wheelchair as she recalled how the sky turned red before the balst ripped off her flesh below the knees.

"We might not have guns, but we have our ambitions and our spirit," Bazazi said in a soft-spoken, determined voice. "Even if it's with our hands and nails, we'll overthrow the regime."

In a report on December 28, 2004, *The Independent* (U.K.) wrote: Tank Girls: the frontline feminists

These women have come from around the world to bring down Iran's ayatollahs. So why were they bombed by the West? Christine Aziz visits their desert HQ.

As the coalition bombs hit the flat salt plains on the northeastern border of Iraq, members of a little known, female-led Iranian army huddled in a bunker... The NLA is the military wing of the National Council of the Resistance of Iran (NCRI), a female-dominated, Iranian parliament-in-exile whose aim is to topple the Islamic fundamentalist regime and replace it with a secular, democratic government. The NCRI is led by a charismatic Iranian, Maryam Rajavi, 53....

Women make up 30 per cent of the NLA, but 70 per cent of the officers are female. The British Army has just one female brigadier, while in the Navy there are four female captains. Rajavi has long encouraged female participation in the army. She argues that, as misogyny is the mainstay of the Iranian government, who better to strike at it than women?

Her female recruits, many of whom had been tortured and imprisoned in Iran, train alongside men in all aspects of frontline battle, including hand-to-hand combat and armoured vehicle operation.

Yet the most important and greatest role women have played has been leading Ashraf through the most dangerous of times when it was the target of the incessant, suppressive terrorist and military attacks by the mullahs and their Iraqi allies. The goal of these attacks and conspiracies was to destroy Ashraf and the PMOI as an organization and to extradite its members to Iran's ruling mullahs.

In 2003, when the United States and its allies attacked Iraq, American and British planes heavily bombed the PMOI centers in Iraq at the behest of the Iranian regime.[3] As a result of these attacks, dozens of members of the opposition, including a number of PMOI women, three of whom were members of the leadership council, were killed.[4]

With the backing of wealthy Iranian exiles, they are preparing for the day when the order comes to march east over the frontier to liberate their land from the mullahs.

The presence of a female-dominated army prepared to fight the mullahs and Iran's Revolutionary Guards is a powerful symbol to all women in the region. Its effectiveness is not in its military might. The fact that the army exists at all is a huge threat to all male-dominated fundamentalist regimes. It shows what women can do.

The women in Ashraf say they don't want to leave until they have overthrown the regime in Iran.

On March 19, 2005, *The Los Angeles Times* published its reporter's report from Ashraf:

MEK members also project a progressive streak and political ethos unusual in the world, much less the Middle East. They're ardent feminists. Women make up 30% of the fighters but hold an outsized number of political and military leadership positions. Women fight on the front lines, and female tank crews and commanders were common back when they still had tanks.

The all-male Unit 8 is led by a woman, Jila Deiham, a matronly former chemical engineer whose husband was executed in Iran for MEK activities and who lives in separate quarters on the unit grounds along with other female officers.

She theorized that the courage and persistence needed for an Iranian woman to break free of both a repressive government and a male-dominated culture bred particularly strong and brave female cadres

"For a woman to take part in the struggle, she has to overcome more obstacles," Deiham said.

Some of the members of her unit say they had a hard time accepting orders from a woman when they first joined the MEK, but all say they now see it as a point of pride

Mohammed Malik, a 21-year-old musician and composer, called female leadership "the masterpiece of our accomplishments."

3. *The Wall Street Journal*, April 17, 2003; *The Washington Post*, April 18, 2003.

4. Massoumeh Pour Eshraq, Mahboobeh Soufaf and Shahin Hatami, three members of the PMOI leadership council who lost their lives in the 2003 bombings.

After 2003, the mullahs infiltrated extensively into Iraq. Buoyed by concessions as a result of the U.S. appeasement policy, they took control of some of the most important aspects of Iraq's political and security apparatus. They used this unhindered influence to step up their conspiracies against Ashraf, which included missile attacks, kidnapping two opposition members, bombing a bus carrying Iraqi workers being transferred from Ashraf (eleven of whom were killed), consecutive explosions at Ashraf's water pumping station and the assassination of 54 liaisons who procured and provided logistical support for the residents of Ashraf, among other atrocities.

On July 28 and 29, 2009, some 2,000 heavily-armed Iraqi policemen and soldiers accompanied by Humvee armored vehicles attacked the city of Ashraf. They opened fire on defenseless citizens and beat them with clubs, iron rods and axes, killing 11 and wounding over 500 in the process. Thirty-six men were taken hostage and subsequently tortured, harassed and mistreated in various prisons in Iraq. They were only returned to Ashraf after a 72-day hunger strike, which put them at the verge of death.

The steadfastness of the women of Ashraf during the course of this major human catastrophe has been commendable. They worked to prevent the killing of their brothers at any price. How was this possible when bullets flew from all sides and axes landed on defenseless heads and arms? The women of Ashraf rushed to the scene of confrontation, joined their hands together and formed a human chain to shield and protect their bleeding brothers. This act resulted in dozens of these brave women becoming wounded. Later on, the men present at the scene reported that if it were not for the women's high morale, tolerance and admirable initiative in that vicious confrontation, there would have been considerably more casualties.

In the next round of attacks on April 8, 2011, which took the form of a massacre, the Iraqi government, at the behest of the ruling mullahs in Tehran, attacked the defenseless residents of Ashraf with armored columns. As a result, 36 people, including 8 women, were martyred and 346 residents were severely wounded. During this extremely brutal attack, assailants driving Humvees ran over and crushed the bodies of 22 residents. Despite all the bloodshed, the women of Ashraf excelled in this confrontation as well. It was proven once again that these women, the pioneering forces of change, are the sources of an unending treasure and guarantors of victory for Iran's century-long struggle for freedom.

Women's leadership amid such complicated and dangerous conditions as those in Ashraf has been tested time and again. Under such circumstances, women's leadership in Ashraf had to neutralize such plots and attacks while avoiding straying from the focus of its struggle against the clerical regime, preserving the strength of the organization under their leadership, and advancing the movement.

Women of Ashraf in resistance against agents of the Iraqi Prime Ministry, July 2009

One cannot help but genuinely admire the pioneering women in Ashraf and Camp Liberty for the role they have played because they were at the helm of the movement at a time when the prospects for victory looked bleak. The balance of power in Iraq and the region was not in their favor and luck was not always on their side. Still, they led the movement at such volatile times and with no past lessons or precedents from which to draw.

Through their vigilance, prudent decision-making, risk-taking and selflessness, these women wove the cloth of endurance at every turn. Women's leadership was put to test in Ashraf and succeeded in the face of great adversity and despite suffering severe blows. This was accomplished with courage, high morale and perseverance.

For this reason, the situation of women in Ashraf had a great impact on Iranian society, particularly on women and young people. Such an impact was made possible because of two important factors: First, Ashraf has been the standard-bearer of change in Iran, owing to 30 years of struggle and by paying the price for overthrowing religious fascism. Secondly, Ashraf enjoys a broad base of support in Iranian society.

This is why we saw that during the upheavals of 2009, the most important slogans of Iranian youths were the same ones that have been chanted by the residents of Ashraf for the past three decades. The situation in Ashraf was living proof that women could successfully hold leadership roles and made the idea of equality predominant among Iranian women.

In Ashraf, women's leadership has even cultivated democracy among the relationships between members of the opposition. In fact, women's leadership in the city's affairs has led to the creation of new humane values.[5]

The men in this movement, who in their struggle against male-dominated culture have reached great heights of their own, played a significant role in the campaign of perseverance due to the collective progress in the realm of humanity. They fulfilled their responsibilities in a splendid fashion shoulder-to-shoulder with women.

The late Rt. Hon. Lord Slynn of Hadley, a great supporter of Ashraf, once said after visiting the Camp: "Those of us who have been to Ashraf will be struck as I was struck by what has been created in Ashraf. It is at Ashraf that much of this attention is directed. What is to be found in Ashraf is a way of life with a commitment to democracy and to peace. Here is a city created with a system of higher education at times at university levels. The world of culture, creativity and music and literature which will be the envy of many countries."[6]

5. General David Phillips was in Ashraf in 2003 during the years that investigations were conducted on PMOI members. General Phillips, who at the time was a colonel, with the responsibility to protect Ashraf City, wrote in his letter in 2005 to Human Rights Watch: "I personally spent a year of my life in Iraq with the responsibility for Camp Ashraf... I was exceptionally impressed with the dedication of the female units. These units were professional and displayed strong support for freedom, democracy and equality for women... I was very impressed specifically by the all female units. I would like my own daughters to someday visit these units for the cultural exchange. Were it not for the ongoing insurgency throughout Iraq, I would sanction my daughter to travel to Camp Ashraf and meet these very dedicated and professional female members of the Mujahedin e Khalq."

6. The Rt. Hon. Lord Gordon Slynn (1930-2009) was one of the most renowned judges on international level. He had headed the European High Court for Justice (Luxembourg). After the U.S. attack on Iraq in 2003 when the situation of Ashraf residents was greatly endangered because of the conspiracies of the clerical regime, Lord Slynn undertook the humanitarian initiative of leading the legal campaign in defense of Ashraf. In the years 2005-2009, he also headed the team of lawyers of the PMOI in their campaign to remove the organization from the terror lists of the U.K. and the European Union and led this campaign to victory. At the same time, he was a great humanitarian, supporting the impoverished and he had founded a number of charity foundations in various countries.

The women of Ashraf can also be seen as a model of emancipation by women in Iraq and other countries in the region. In June 2006, when 5.2 million Iraqis signed a declaration in support of Ashraf against the religious fascist regime ruling Iran, Iraqi women comprised 700,000 of the signatories.

The activities of the women of Ashraf over the past three decades have served as an inspiration to the women and youths struggling to achieve freedom and equality in Iran. For the past thirty years, the Iranian resistance has launched a full-fledged war against the ruling religious fascism in Iran. This backward and reactionary regime is based on gender apartheid and utilizes the most modern techniques in attempting to suppress the populace and enforce censorship. It also employs state-sponsored terrorism accompanied by an extensive misinformation campaign to create an atmosphere of fear and terror. Above all, it exploits religious sentiments. All of this combined has resulted in a truly new phenomenon in history.

Standing up to this source of darkness and countering its evil would not have been possible unless every part of this resistance had not been infused with the most fundamental of human values, namely, equality, freedom, freedom of choice and democracy. It is with such a mindset that the one thousand brave and selfless women of Ashraf have remained steadfast in their campaign against the clerical regime.

Now, we shall see how women's leadership in the Iranian resistance has been tested during trying times and how it has proven successful.

FACTORS CONTRIBUTING TO PERSEVERANCE

How did the perseverance of the residents of Ashraf become possible? What were the contributing factors and from where did they emanate?

This steadfastness was made possible through a tireless struggle for equality. In other words, it was the outcome of a ceaseless demarcation between equality and inequality, between human emancipation and captivity. Overcoming the seemingly insurmountable challenges that human beings face in today's world would be impossible without a commitment to gender equality. Discovering this truth was the result of years of struggle against the misogynist mullahs' regime, a struggle that evolved into a fundamental cultural transformation in the People's Mojahedin Organization of Iran (PMOI/ MEK) in the 1980s.

Massoud Rajavi, the Leader of the Iranian resistance, described this revolution as one that drew a clear boundary against the ideology of the mullahs and other reactionaries. He reiterated that its aim was to "cast aside gender-based exploitation, symbolized by the mullahs and the regime's Islamic Revolutionary Guards." Indeed, it was Masoud's vision and the ideals that rejects exploitation which he defends that increasingly paved the way for women's struggle for equality. The PMOI made the significant discovery that if it were to stand against religious tyranny, then it had to fight each and every ideological and cultural remnant of fundamentalism.

In a nutshell, we realized that the eradication of gender-based ideology frees a tremendous amount of energy within the resistance movement itself. It generates an astounding dynamism that enables enormous strides, which could then serve as the source of our power. This transformation brought with it an incredible treasure trove of human experiences. At this point, it would be helpful to discuss the four most significant building blocks of this transformation.

The first change was women's active participation in the resistance's leadership and decision-making positions at all levels, the details of which have been elucidated above. Today, we see efforts being made around the world aimed at increasing women's role in political and economic management, which is valuable in its own right. The experience of the Iranian resistance, however, shows that the ultimate and definitive solution for breaking the spell of inequality is only achievable through a profound leap forward. Women's hegemony in the Iranian resistance, as a foundation-shattering transformation, paved the way for women to take on crucial responsibilities, gain invaluable expertise and hone their abilities in all fields.

Another major development was that many of the women and men of the resistance voluntarily sacrificed a normal family life, consciously separated from their spouses and concentrated all their energies, emotions, power and attention on the struggle at hand. The prerequisite for engaging in this full-time struggle was to forego the comfort and tranquility of a normal life and everything that accompanied it. Otherwise, women could not have positioned themselves at the heart of this formidable battle against religious fascism, let alone assume leadership responsibilities.

Prior to this decision, members of the resistance led normal lives with their families in various centers in Iraq. Their children had attended kindergartens and schools that were set up in Ashraf and family life had not yet become an impediment to active engagement in the struggle. Since the early 1990s, however, the security situation in Iraq deteriorated drastically and to the great detriment of the PMOI. Iraq was engulfed in war and the PMOI was the target of continuous bombings and terrorist attacks. For this reason, it became impossible for the families to congregate in Ashraf or other PMOI bases. PMOI members had two options: abandon their full-time struggle and leave the area, or sacrifice everything to keep the flames of the resistance burning. In reality, members of the resistance took the struggle against fundamentalism to new heights, choosing to forego family attachments. One can only imagine how difficult this would be for any human being.

The third development was the establishment of new democratic relations within the ranks of the resistance. This movement, by virtue of making significant strides in the realm of gender equality, has succeeded in creating an environment within itself that is conducive to elevating democratic relations to higher levels. This has led to an atmosphere where transparency, honesty and criticism among individuals could thrive and various viewpoints and opinions could be freely exchanged. When a number of people gather together for the common cause of freedom, their own relationships, first and foremost, must necessarily be based on the principle of democracy and free choice.

Forming such relations in the midst of a thorny and demanding struggle against a formidable enemy is not an easy task. Incidentally, for a movement subjected to the harshest forms of suppression, it is imperative to have internal unity and for every individual to accept responsibility. The precondition for building such bonds is freedom and democracy within the organization. The resistance movement responded to these imperatives by forming novel human relationships, which can be seen, for example, in the course of numerous meetings held by people working closely together or in the same department. In addition to the meetings organized for coordination of activities or political discussions, there are also meetings in which reciprocal constructive criticisms could be voiced.

Finally, the fourth development has been the rise of a new generation of men who believe deeply in the ideal of gender equality. In the course of a profound transformation, they have rid their thinking and behavior of the old culture while overcoming and defeating the ideology that perceives women as objects.

In their regular meetings, they engage in a cultural and ideological struggle to distance themselves from this distorted ideology. In both their thoughts and deeds, they see women as equal human beings.

Free from a gender-based ideology, they attempt to see the positive qualities of women and as equal human beings. They, therefore, strive to recognize and discover women as independent, equal, free and emancipated beings.

After this cultural transformation took place, these men have found themselves experiencing a higher intellectual realm marked by a belief in equality throughout the course of their activities and responsibilities. This means that men in the resistance realize that in the absence of equality, half of the energy and creativity would vanish. Therefore, when it comes to the evaluation of expertise and practical skills, they refuse to judge women by the old yardsticks. This is because they realize that in the realm of work and responsibility, these women harbor new and modern methods and values. As a matter of fact, if men recognize and learn these methods and values, it would lead to a greater wealth of creativity, dynamism, speed and capability for them as well. Men in the resistance can and do develop a new attitude which helps them recognize women's strengths as human beings.

EMERGENCE OF THE HUMAN ESSENCE AND POWERS

The process by which women began to occupy leadership positions was, of course, a very difficult one in Ashraf and in the resistance movement in general. Its progress and evolution, however, brought to the fore new capacities and powers in the personalities of each and every member of the resistance, particularly women. The women of PMOI have achieved many of the ideals of the equality movement. Their experience can only be described with the help of such terms as "rebirth," "the creation of a new culture," and "human epics."

Once women experienced how valuable their independent and responsible role could be in advancing the cause of the struggle against religious tyranny, they abandoned the irresponsible and passive world of a woman who identifies herself through a man. By doing so, they assumed the role of a responsible woman tasked with leading a struggle with all its attendant consequences.

After assuming leadership positions and realizing that they must utilize all their might to achieve their objectives, women recognized that they had to undergo change all the time; that they needed to continuously learn and teach, and that they needed to constantly discover new ways and methods for carrying out their work. They had effectively entered a new world governed by new laws, in which stagnation, immobility and the inability to move forward was tantamount to a regression to the old world they had left behind. They had stepped into a world where if they failed to resolve its existing problems and contradictions every minute of the day, they would eventually regress. Therefore, indecisiveness gave way to resolve and facing hardships head on became part of the enduring spirit. These women have overcome extreme adversity and unforeseen developments. For them, accepting responsibilities is unconditional, bold and unlimited; they face all kinds of threats and their consequences directly. In preparing themselves for every worst-case scenario, they have heightened their potentials and capabilities.

They are convinced that there is a solution for every hardship and roadblock. It is only the enemy that wants to portray everything as impossible, all doors closed and humankind as weak and powerless. That is why the enemy, Iran's ruling mulllahs, is extremely terrified of these women. When they have a difference of opinion, their principal value is to strive to identify the root cause of the problem and find a way out of it instead of simply reacting to others' views.

They have reached such a high level of human dignity that even when confronted with negative behavior or comments, they do not automatically reciprocate. They have learned not to focus on the individual characters and the behavior of their interlocutors, but instead exhibit tolerant behavior and patience. These qualities enable them to concentrate on the root causes that when ignored give way to antagonism and foster counterproductive rancor. This is a giant step forward in the exaltation of social relations that, if expanded in scope, would lead to an energetic and united world where only sisterly and brotherly solidarity would reign. Fortunately, this trait has also taken root among the men of the resistance.

The women in the PMOI have also developed the power to markedly increase their love for their fellow human beings. This has helped them to think of others before all else, and their first priority, which they contemplate and find solutions for, is to discover ways to help, teach, and better organize a greater number of their sisters to pave the way for their advancement. They teach them how to solve complicated and multifaceted problems in the departments that they are tasked to lead. These noble values have enabled them to form, organize and teach a united and harmonious society of women who are ready to tackle the most demanding responsiblities in all fields.

This is truly a new phenomenon in the social evolution of humankind. This element is imperative to the healthy functioning of even the most advanced societies and helps them reach acceptable levels of democracy and progress. In social developments, the heart of the problem lies in the contradiction between the interests of the individual and society at large. The complexity of this problem rests in the fact that the correct solution varies in each case and there exists no general formula to cover all cases. Instead, in each case there is a judgment that is made regarding which party must forgo what it perceives to be its 'right.'

The women of the resistance have learned through experience that in cooperative endeavors, the correct solution is to always give priority to the interests of their sisters. This would open the way for the participation of women at all levels in the management of society.

These women have pledged not to abandon the ideals of freedom, democracy and equality under any circumstances. They have vowed to fight tyranny and dictatorship in all its forms and are ready to pay the price, whatever it may be. They are prepared to sacrifice their flesh and bones, their affection for their families and to endure even the hardships of undergoing a change of culture, especially a change from a patriarchal regime.

The generation of men in the Iranian resistance, who were responsible for creating an unparalleled value system by remaining committed to the ideal of equality and by distancing themselves from the male-dominated culture, should be commended. By adopting a mindset that sees people not in terms of their genders but as equal human beings, they have unearthed their own true human identity.

OUR MESSAGE

If this century is the century for women's emancipation, all political, economic, social and cultural progress must walk along this path. The emancipation of women is the most pressing issue of our times. We, in the Iranian resistance, realized the need for women's emancipation on the path to resolve the problems of our country, the most pressing of which were the overthrow of religious tyranny and the establishment of freedom and democracy. We ended up needing to liberate women both to gain victory over the regime and to guarantee the future freedom and prosperity of Iran. Peace, progress and democracy are contingent upon women's emancipation, equality and leadership. Ignoring or neglecting this reality will inevitably aggravate the situation and contribute to war, violence, dictatorship and retrogression.

The 21st century, the century for women's freedom and the elimination of discrimination against them, the century for peace, progress and democracy, is unfolding. At the same time, the fundamentalists and reactionaries, who are being resurrected from the depths of the Dark Ages, are trying to turn back the wheels of history through their misogyny. They do not realize that in many parts of the world, including in Iran, they will be swept from the pages of history by the powerful hands of free and liberated women. This is the historic mandate of the free women of our time. In the absence of it, human society and civilization would remain exposed to the threat posed by reactionaries. Without a doubt, the antithesis the misogynous fundamentalists and reactionaries are the free women who will rise up hand in hand against them. In the shadow of their growing resistance, they will realize women's emancipation everywhere and herald the liberation of all humankind.

This is the dawn of the greatest development in human history and society. Let us welcome it with hope and faith.

Appendix 1:
Women's freedoms and equality in tomorrow's Iran

On February 23, 2010, in a meeting at the European Parliament entitled, "Women, Pioneers of Democratic Change in Iran," Mrs. Maryam Rajavi shared her views on women's freedom and equality in tomorrow's Iran. The following text was distributed among the MEPs and other audience members at the meeting.

Some of these views had been previously announced by Mrs. Rajavi on various occasions in preceding years.

***

Honoring thousands upon thousands of heroines who have been executed over the past three decades for resisting Iran's ruling religious fascism;

Saluting the pioneering women in the resistance against the clerical regime who assumed key roles, especially the one thousand female pioneers in Ashraf;

Admiring the courageous women of Iran who stood at the frontlines of the upheaval against the misogynous dictatorship beginning in June 2009;

Adhering to the principle of separation of church and state adopted as a plan in 1985 by the National Council of Resistance of Iran and the NCRI's plan on Rights and Freedoms of Women adopted in 1987;

Recalling the Iranian resistance's commitment to annulling the death penalty after toppling the clerical regime in Iran, announced in 2005;

Reiterating that the misogynous laws and medieval punishments practiced by the religious tyranny in Iran under the name of Islam run contrary to the truth of Islam and its message of tolerance and compassion;

Emphasizing that the international documents relevant to human rights and women's rights–specifically the Universal Declaration on Human Rights, the Convention to Eliminate All Forms of Discrimination Against Women, the Declaration on the Elimination of Violence Against Women, the International Covenants on Civil and Political Rights, the International Convention on Economic, Social and Cultural rights, and Convention Against Torture and Inhumane and Humiliating Treatment or Punishment–will be respected by the civil code in tomorrow's Iran;

We emphasize the following issues regarding the freedoms and equality of women in tomorrow's Iran:

1. Fundamental freedoms and rights

- Women shall have the equal right to enjoy all human rights and fundamental freedoms;

- Irrespective of their ethnicity, religion, social class or demographics, women everywhere, in whatever village or city, must have the same rights as men in all economic, social and political spheres. Discrimination[1] against women must be abolished in all its forms.

- Women are free to choose their place of residence, occupation, and education. They must have the ability to choose their spouse and clothing, travel freely have the right to leave the country, to obtain foreign citizenship, to devolve citizenship to their children, to divorce, and to obtain custody of children.

- Women should not be degraded based on their belief in a specific faith or religion, nor should it prevent them from access to employment opportunities or educational and judicial resources.

2. Equality before the law

- Women must enjoy protection under the law equal to men.

- Women must enjoy access to guaranteed judicial recourse in the face of violence, rape, discrimination and deprivation of liberty.

- Women must have the same rights as men before the courts.

- Courts must view testimonies and affidavits submitted by women as equal in importance as those submitted by men.

- The legal age for girls shall be 18. They shall not have full criminal responsibility before the age of 18.

---

1. The Convention on the Elimination of All Forms of Discrimination against Women, Article 1: The term "discrimination against women" shall mean any distinction, exclusion or restriction made on the basis of sex which has the effect or purpose of impairing or nullifying the recognition, enjoyment or exercise by women, irrespective of their marital status, on a basis of equality of men and women, of human rights and fundamental freedoms in the political, economic, social, cultural, civil or any other field.

3. Freedom of choosing one's own clothing

- Women must be free to choose their own clothing. Government interference in this regard should be prohibited.

- The law of forced veiling shall be repealed.[2]

- Laws that prescribe administrative punishment for female workers' lack of veiling shall be repealed. [3]

- Written or unwritten laws on controlling the clothing or behavior of women under the rubric of "mal-veiling," which have violated Iranian women's right to freedom and security, shall have no place in tomorrow's Iran.

4. Equal participation in political leadership

- Women shall enjoy the right to participate "in the formulation of government policy and the implementation thereof and to hold public office and perform all public functions at all levels of government."[4]

- Women must specifically enjoy the right to equal participation in the country's political leadership.

- In order to dispense with any inequality, I will propose that the government appoint women for at least half of its posts. I

---

2. Article 638, Islamic Punishment Law, adopted in 1996: "Anyone who openly engages in forbidden acts in public or public places will receive punishment proportional to the act in addition to imprisonment ranging from 10 days to two months or up to 74 lashes. In the event that they commit an act which essentially has no attributed punishment but nonetheless tarnishes public morals, the punishment shall only be imprisonment ranging from 10 days to two months or up to 74 lashes."

Amendment: "Women who appear without Sharia veiling in public and public places will be sentenced to imprisonment ranging from 10 days to two months or monetary penalties ranging from 50,000 to 500,000 rials."

3. Paragraph 20 of Article 8 of the laws on "Examination of Administrative Offenses" (ratified in 1993) considers women's failure to comply with forcible veiling as an "administrative offense," which carries punishments such as written warnings or in some cases even dismissal from work.

4. The Convention on the Elimination of All Forms of Discrimination against Women

will also propose that political parties choose women for least half their candidates for parliamentary elections.

- Any laws that cause prohibitions or limitations on women occupying government posts or senior judicial and legal positions must be repealed.

5. Equality in the economic sphere

- Women shall enjoy equal rights as men in terms of inheritance, entering contracts and management of property.

- Women shall have equal opportunities as men in the labor market.[5]

- Women must receive equal pay for the same work as men, in addition to job security and full benefits.

- In accessing housing, appropriate nutrition, medical services and employment, as well as athletic and artistic endeavors, women shall enjoy equal opportunities as men.

6. Equality in the family

- Women must have free and equal rights to choose, marry or divorce a spouse.

- Polygamy shall be prohibited.

- Marriage before a legal age shall be prohibited.

- Familial responsibilities such as housekeeping, raising children, employment, and educating children shall be the obligation of both men and women.

- Women shall have the right to obtain custody over their children.

---

5. Women comprise only 12 percent of the work force in Iran.

- Employment of girls younger than the legal age shall be prohibited. They shall enjoy special privileges in the field of education.

- Government inquisition and interference in the private life of women shall be prohibited.

7. Prohibition of violence

- Various forms of violence[6] against women, acts of intimidation or forcible deprivation of their freedoms shall be considered a crime.

8. Pohibition of gender exploitation

- Sex trade shall be prohibited.

- Trafficking of women and forcing them into prostitution shall be a crime and those responsible shall be criminally prosecuted.[7]

---

6. Declaration on the Elimination of Violence against Women, Article 2:

Violence against women shall be understood to encompass, but not be limited to, the following:

(a)   Physical, sexual and psychological violence occurring in the family, including battering, sexual abuse of female children in the household, marital rape, female genital mutilation and other additional practices harmful to women, non-spousal violence and violence related to exploitation;

(b)   Physical, sexual and psychological violence occurring within the general community, including rape, sexual abuse, sexual harassment and intimidation at work, in educational institutions and elsewhere, trafficking in women and forced prostitution;

(c)   Physical, sexual and psychological violence perpetrated or condoned by the State, wherever it occurs.

7. Excerpts from the US State Department's 2009 Trafficking in Persons Report (TIP): "Iran is a source, transit, and destination for men, women, and children trafficked for the purposes of sexual exploitation and involuntary servitude. Iranian women are trafficked internally for the purpose of forced prostitution and forced marriage. Iranian and Afghan children living in Iran are trafficked internally for the purpose of forced marriage, commercial sexual exploitation, and involuntary servitude as beggars or laborers to pay debts, provide income, or support drug addiction of their families. Iranian women and girls are also trafficked to Pakistan, Turkey, Qatar, Kuwait, the United Arab Emirates, Iraq, France, Germany, and the United Kingdom for commercial sexual exploitation... The law permits temporary marriage for a fixed term ("sigheh"), after which the marriage is terminated. Some persons abuse this institution in order to coerce women into sexual exploitation; there are reports of Iranian women sold into

- Anyone committing sexual crimes against children shall be prosecuted.

- Any exploitation of women under any pretext is prohibited. All traditions, laws and regulations according to which the parents, a guardian or anyone else putting girls or women at the disposal of others on the pretext of marriage or any other pretext for sexual gratification or exploitation shall be repealed.[8]

9. Repealing mullahs' Sharia laws

- The mullahs' Sharia laws shall not have a place in the laws of the future Iran.

- Emphasis shall be "to repeal all national penal provisions which constitute discrimination against women."[9]

- Appalling and brutal laws such as stoning shall be repealed.

- All laws authorizing crimes against women under familial pre-texts shall be repealed.

10. Social benefits

- Women must have access to social benefits, especially as they relate to retirement, unemployment, old age and other forms of disability, in addition to the right to maternity leave during

---

fixed term marriages to men from Pakistan and Gulf states or into forced prostitution. It was extremely difficult for women forced into sexual exploitation to obtain justice: first, because the testimony of two women is equal to that of one man, and second, because women who are victims of sexual abuse are vulnerable to being executed for adultery, defined as sexual relations outside marriage… The government reportedly punishes victims for unlawful acts committed as a result of being trafficked, for example, adultery and prostitution. There were reports that the government arrested, prosecuted, and punished several trafficking victims on charges of prostitution or adultery." (pp. 161-162)

8. The National Council of Resistance of Iran: Plan for Women's Freedoms and Rights, ratified on April 17, 1987

9. The Convention on the Elimination of All Forms of Discrimination against Women

pregnancy and after delivery, and the right to sufficient nutrition and free services during this period.

- The government should plan for providing nursery and day care for the children of working women.

- All employed women should have access to nursery and day care centers for their children.

- Minority women, female refugees or immigrants, women living in villages or remote areas, underprivileged women, female prisoners, young girls, and disabled or weak or old women, shall enjoy special financial, educational and medical support from the government.

- Depriving women employed under temporary contracts of social benefits shall be prohibited.

- Dismissing women from work or reducing their wages due to pregnancy or delivery, or obligating them to perform harmful jobs during this period shall be prohibited.

- Responsibility for supporting single women who provide for their families shall be a necessary task of the government.[10]

---

10. This expression is used for women who are the sole breadwinners for families that in some instances are comprised of older parents or several children. These women have either lost their husbands or have divorced, or are married but their husbands are on the run, addicted to drugs, in prison, unemployed, immigrants or disabled. Such families are among the poorest sectors of society in Iran.

According to a 2006 census in Iran, the number of such households was 1.641.000 at the time. But on December 22, 2009, a government official told the media that the number had reached two million.

Appendix 2:
Mullahs' Misogynous Laws

The oppression of women is deeply enshrined in various sections of the clerical regime's laws. The constitution, laws, civil code, punishment law, ecomonic, administrative and cultural laws are deeply influenced by male-domination and the most fundamental rights and freedoms of women have been trampled.

The constitution of the *Velayat-e Faqih* regime has conditioned women's equality on the observance of "Islamic" standards.

According to Article 20, "All members of the nation, both men and women, enjoy equal support of the law and enjoy all human, political, economic, social and cultural rights provided that Islamic standards are observed."

And according to Article 21, "The government is obliged to guarantee women's rights in all respects while observing Islamic standards."

Since the ruling mullahs follow a fundamentalist interpretation that is in fact misogynous, their outlook and laws are based on the oppression of women and discrimination against them.

According to the laws ratified by the mullahs since 1979–on marriage, divorce, employment, choice of place of residence, comings and goings, departure from country, etc.–women are doomed to follow the decisions and permissions of men. Girls' marriage is conditioned on "the father's permission." If a father wants, he can wed his daughter before 13 years of age with the court's permission.

In these laws, the age of marriage for girls has been considered 13. Men's hegemony in the family is absolute. Divorce is the monopolized right of men. According to the law, by marrying a man, a woman is obliged to abide by his wishes and be prepared to have sexual relations with him whenever he wishes. Parenthood (including guardianship, financial affairs, deciding on education, place of residence, permission to leave the country, allowing medical treatment, etc.) is the father's right and not the mother's. According to the law, the father's parenthood and guardianship is "mandatory." This means that even if the father wants, he cannot relegate the responsibility to his wife.

According to these laws, men can have four official wives and numerous temporary ones.

The age for penal accountability is eight years and nine months for girls and 14 years and six months for boys. Therefore, if a 9-year-old girl commits a crime, she will be dealt with as an adult.

These laws also compel women to observe the government's dress code. They set a woman's share of inheritance at half the man's. In some cases, women's testimony before the court is prohibited. These laws back murder of women by men under the pretext of honor killing.

In addition, women are deprived of running for presidency or sitting on the bench to judge.

The mullahs' laws are noteworthy with regard to misogyny from several respects:

Since misogyny is inherent to the *Veleyat-e Faqih* regime, the laws regarding women are generally the unalterable part of the mullahs' law.

As a result, the laws ratified against women under the mullahs' rule have not been altered. On the contrary, they have become more voluminous and more pervasive.

The practices concerning women in the courts of justice, police centers and work and living environments are more hostile than the regime's law, particularly since Article 61 of the Constitution obliges the Judiciary to "take action based on divine laws" and Article 167 allows judges to issue their decrees by citing "credible Islamic sources or credible decrees." This article paves the way for enforcement of the most misogynous medieval rulings vindicated in the mullahs' religious laws.

The following are some articles from the misogynous laws of the clerical regime:

WOMEN'S OPPRESSION IN THE FAMILY

Article 1105 of the Civil Code: "In the relationship between husband and wife, heading the family is the characteristic of the husband. The Council of Guardians of the Constitution has declared that a woman does not have the right to leave her home without her husband's permission, not even to attend her father's funeral."

Article 489 of the Islamic Punishment Law: "Whenever a woman has a miscarriage, she must pay its bloodmoney (*diyah*) at whatever stage it happens and she is not entitled to any share of it."

Article 1108 of the Civil Code: "Whenever a woman refrains from performing her duty in sexual relations, she will not be entitled to her allowance."

MARRIAGE AND DIVORCE BASED ON VIOLATIONS OF WOMEN'S RIGHTS

Article 1133 of the Civil Code allows a man to divorce his wife whenever he wishes.

Article 1043 of the Civil Code: "Marriage of virgin girls is conditioned on the permission of the father or the father's father."

Article 1059 of the Civil Code forbids women from marrying "non-Muslim" men.

MEN'S POLYGAMY

Article 1048 of the Civil Code: "Marrying two sisters is forbidden even if it is done in intervals."

Article 1049 of the Civil Code: "No one can marry the daughter of his brother-in-law or the daughter of his sister-in-law unless his wife allows."

Article 900 of the Civil Code: "One quarter of the inheritance is the share of the wife or wives in the event the husband dies without children."

Article 901 of the Civil Code: "One-eighth is the share of the wife or wives in the event the husband dies with children."

STONING

Articles 102 to 105 of the penal code (The Islamic Punishment Law) on stoning:

Article 102: "At the time of stoning, men must be buried up to the waist and women till the chest, and then stoned."

Article 103: "Whenever a person condemned to stoning runs away from the ditch, he must be returned for the punishment to be carried out if his adultery has been proven by testimony; if his adultery has been proven by his own confession, he will not be returned."

Article 104: "The size of the stones used for stoning should not be so large to kill the convict with a couple of hits and not too small such that they could not be called stones."

BANNED FROM JUDGESHIP AND PRESIDENCY

According to the regime's laws, women cannot become presidents or judges.

The mullahs' Constitution considers in Article 115 that presidency is only the right of "religious and political men."

Article 163 of the Constitution conditions qualifications of a judge on the mullahs' "religious standards": "The requirements and qualifications of a judge are determined by law based on religious standards."

In "the Law of Conditions of Selecting Justice Ministry Judges" (adopted April 1982), it is said, "Judges must be selected from among men who have the following qualifications: 1. Faith, justice and commitment in practice to Islamic standards and loyalty to the Islamic Republic of Iran…"

In 1985, with reforms in the abovesaid law, women could take up positions of consultants or investigative judges in judicial authorities. However, they are deprived of the right to write the verdict.

UNJUST SHARE OF INHERITANCE

In the Iranian law under the mullahs' rule, women's share of the inheritance is set as half the share of men's. This corellation dominates all the articles of the Civil Code regarding inheritance.

According to Article 947 of the Civil Code, women can only inherit from transportable belongings. This means that women cannot inherit lands or gardens.

Article 913 of the Civil Code: "If a man has children, his wife can inherit one-eighth of his belongings. If he does not have children, the wife can inherit one-fourth. But if a woman does not have any other inheritors, her husband inherits all her belongings. And if she has other inheritors, half of her belongings go to her husband. If the husband does not have any inheritors, one-fourth of his belongings go to his wife and the rest go to the government."

Article 907 of the Civil Code: "When the father and mother who have daughters and sons die, sons inherit twice the daughters."

DEPRIVED OF CHILDREN'S CUSTODY

Article 1180 of the Civil Code: "The minor child is under mandatory guardianship of the father or grandfather on the father's side."

Article 1169 of the Civil Code: "In the custody of children, the mother has priority for two years after the child's birth. After this time, the child's custody is with the father except children who are under the custody of the mother until seven years of age."

Article 1170 of the Civil Code: "If the mother marries while having the child's custody, the custody will go to the father."

MANDATORY VEILING

Article 638 of the Islamic Punishment Law: "Anyone who explicitly violates any religious taboo in public beside being punished for the act should also be imprisoned from ten days to two months, or should be flogged (74 lashes).

"Note- women who appear in public without a proper *hijab* should be imprisoned from ten days to two months or pay a fine of 50,000 to 500,000 Ryal."

SANCTIONING CRIMES AGAINST WOMEN

Article 209 of the Islamic Punishment Law: "Whenever a Muslim man deliberately kills a Muslim woman, he is condemned to retribution but the parent of the (killled) woman must pay the (killer) man half of his blood money before retribution of the murderer."

Article 220 of the Islamic Punishment Law: "The father or the father's father who kills his child is not entitled to retribution but will be sentenced to payment of the (child's) blood money to the inheritors of the murdered victim and to imprisonment."

Article 226 of the Islamic Punishment Law: "Homicide is allowed retribution if the murdered is religiously not worthy of killing. And if he/she is worthy of murder, the murderer must prove the worth based on standards in the court."

According to Article 630 of the Islamic Punishment Law, the husband can kill his wife for having relations with another man and he can be exonerated for this reason.

Article 300 of the Islamic Punishment Law: "The blood money for the first- or second-degree murder of a Muslim woman is half that of a murdered Muslim man."

Deprived from choice of employment

Article 1117 of the Civil Code: "The husband can prohibit his wife from any profession or industry that contradicts family interests, his own dignity or hers."

MANDATORY RESIDENCE

Article 1114 of the Civil Code: "The woman must reside in the house that her husband specifies unless the right to specify has been relegated to the wife."

TWO WOMEN'S TESTIMONY EQUALS ONE MAN'S

Article 237 of the Islamic Punishment Law: "Deliberate murder is proven by the testimonies of two just men (women's testimony is not accounted for at all)... Quasi-intentional or unintentional murder is proven by the testimonies of two just men or one just man and two just women."

Article 189 of the Islamic Punishment Law: "Waging war (on God) and corrupting Earth are proven by the testimony of two just men and the testimony of women does not have any value."

Article 170 of the Islamic Punishment Law: "To prove that somebody has drunk wine, only the testimonies of two just men are acceptable and the testimony of women is not accepted."

PAINFUL DESTINY OF GIRL CHILDREN

Article 1210 of the Civil Code- Amendment 1: "The age of puberty is 9 lunar years for girls (8 solar years and 9 months). For boys it is 15 lunar years, i.e. 14 solar years and six months."

Article 49 of the Islamic Punishment A: "Children are exonerated from punishment if they commit a crime and their rehabilitation is assumed under the supervision of the court by the child's custodian and if necessary, any child rehabilitation center."

Note 1 – Child refers to the person who has not reached the religious age of maturity. (According to this law, if a girl child commits a crime, since she is considered mature according to the mullahs' religion, she will be dealt with as an adult and all the legal punishments like flogging, execution and even stoning can be issued for her.)

In Note 1 of Article 1210 of the Civil Code, it is stated that, "the age of maturity is 15 lunar years for boys and nine lunar years for girls." In light of Article 1041 of the same code, which bans "marriage before the age of maturity," this note sanctions the forced marriage of girl children even under 9 years of age.

Appendix 3:
Mullahs' Enmity to CEDAW

The Convention on the Elimination of All Forms of Discrimination (CEDAW) was ratified almost simultaneously with the beginning of *Velayat-e Faqih* rule in Iran. In September 1981, once the number of signatory governments reached the quorum, it became binding for the governments that had joined it.

The clerical regime's inherent opposition to the basic contents of this convention on the one hand, and the growing universal credibility of the convention on the other, turned the CEDAW into a challenge for the Iranian regime. The enormous and powerful yearning in Iranian society for equality had placed the mullahs in dire straits. Nevertheless, the mullahs ignored the consequences of their decision and officially announced their opposition to the CEDAW in the 1990s.

According to a report provided by the government delegation committee, only Article 1 of this convention contradicted 90 articles in the clerical regime's Constitution, the Civil Code, the Islamic Punishment Law, etc. Taking note of this report as well as the report by Women's Social-Cultural Council, the Supreme Council for Cultural Revolution opposed joining the convention.

The regime's rejection of this convention happened at a time when a mullah by the name of Khatami became president of the regime with claims of reform and moderation. Khatami approved the regime's refusal to join the CEDAW which served his true mandate, i.e. defending the *Velayat-e Faqih*. The decision was made in the Supreme Council for Cultural Revolution presided by Khatami in its 413th session on January 24, 1998.[1]

The ruling mullahs also tried to cite reactionary and medieval interpretations of Islam to pretend that the contents of this convention contradicted Islam and religion, so that they could counter the wave of the equality movement in Iranian society, especially the efforts and struggles of Iranian women.

Here you can see a selection of the most important decrees issued by state-supported Ayatollahs, including the mullahs' leader Ali Khamenei, who have opposed the CEDAW.[2]

Question – According to Article 1 of the CEDAW any form of distinction, exception and/or restriction based on gender in political, economic, social, cultural, civil, etc. grounds must be annulled... Is women's equality with men in the said respects compatible with religious laws?

---

1. The text of the ratified document is as follows: "On the Islamic Republic of Iran's refusal to join the Convention on Elimination of All Forms of Discrimination – Doc No 4868. February 25, 1998

The document ratified in the 413th session on February 3, 1998 of the Supreme Council for Cultural Revolution, following the document adopted in the 395th session of the Supreme Council on designation of a delegation to study the Islamic Republic of Iran's joining the CEDAW, the letter dated October 13, 1997 by the delegation's secretary was discussed and the Supreme Council disagreed with the Islamic Republic of Iran's joining the convention.

Signed: President (of the republic) and head of the Supreme Council for Cultural Revolution – Seyed Mohammad Khatami"

2. These views were published in 1997 by the Research Center of the state-run radio and television network under the title, "Questions from the Grand Leadership and Grand Ayatollahs Tabrizi, Makarem Shirazi, Safi, Mazaheri and Nouri Hamedani." The collection shows that CEDAW contradicts 40 religious rulings and 70 local laws.

Ayatollah Khamenei:

Women's equality with men in this regard is not compatible with the sacred religious rulings of Islam.

Ayatollah Makarem Shirazi:

Without a doubt, complete equality is not only against the requirements of the Shiite religion but also against the requirements of Islam and against the letter of the Quran and the subsequent narrations...

Ayatollah Tabrizi:

Women's equality with men in the said regards is incompatible with the sacred rulings of the religion.

Ayatollah Mazaheri:

The above-said are not compatible with religious laws.

Ayatollah Safi:

In the said cases and some others, women's equality with men is not compatible with the rulings of the sacred religion.

Question: Considering that Article 9 and section 4 of Article 15 view women and men as equal with regards to business, travel, alteration or preservation of one's own and children's nationality, is a woman allowed to become the natural citizen of any country or reside in any city without the agreement of her husband?

Ayatollah Khamenei:

The choice of place of residence and living abides by the views of the man unless a different condition is set in the marriage contract.

Ayatollah Makarem Shirazi:

This is one of the cases referred to above and is not compatible with Islamic culture and rulings. In addition, there is no doubt that this will become the source of much vice in human society...

Ayatollah Tabrizi:

The choice of place of residence (and consequently one's nationality) is that of man unless the woman specifies a special place of residence as a condition in the marriage contract, in which case, the man must comply with the said condition.

Ayatollah Mazaheri:

She cannot (do so) and the husband's permission is required.

Ayatollah Safi:

She cannot.

Question: Is a woman able to leave home with her husband's permission for economic, political or social activities?

Ayatollah Khamenei:

It is not permissible for a woman to leave home without the consent and permission of her husband, although legitimate activities are allowed within her own limits.

Ayatollah Makarem Shirazi:

If it does not contradict the rights of the husband, she probably could. And if she has set such a right for herself (as a condition) in the marriage contract, then certainly there is no problem.

Ayatollah Tabrizi:

Even if leaving home does not contradict the husband's right, the wife cannot leave home without the husband's permission...